The Future of Welfare

The Future
of Welfare

The Social Market Foundation

February 1998

First published by The Social Market Foundation 1998
in association with Profile Books Ltd

The Social Market Foundation
11 Tufton Street
London SW1P 3QB

Profile Books
62 Queen Anne Street
London W1M 9LA

Printed in Great Britain by Watkiss Studios Ltd

A CIP catalogue record for this book is available from the British Library

Paper No. 35

ISBN 1 874097 127

Contents

Contributors

ANTHONY PAUL COLES is Senior Adviser to Mayor Rudolph W. Giuliani of
the City of New York. He oversees the City's Workfare and capital projects
programmes, co-ordinates the implementation of welfare legislation and is
responsible for developing new ways of delivering public services through
managed competition, privatisation and public/private partnerships. A former
Office of the United States and Litigation Attorney, he has also served as Mayor
Giuliani's Deputy Counsel.

PETER COVE is one of America's leading advocates for private solutions to
welfare dependency. After holding key posts in New York City municipal
government, in 1984 he founded America Works, an award winning private
company linking private-sector investment and employment with welfare reform.
In a unique arrangement with states and cities, America Works is paid only where
it successfully delivers a person from welfare into work.

EVAN DAVIS has been an Economics Correspondent at the BBC since 1993.
Now at *Newsnight*, he has worked to dispel misconceptions on major economic
themes such as the changing jobs market and competitiveness. He previously held
research jobs at the Institute for Fiscal Studies and at the London Business School.
A member of the SMF's Advisory Council, his papers include *Schools and the State*
and *The Importance of Resource Accounting*.

FRANK FIELD has been MP for Birkenhead since 1979 and was appointed
Minister for Welfare Reform in May 1997. A former Frontbench Spokesman on
education and social security, he is also Chair of the Social Security Select
Committee. He recently produced a paper for the SMF entitled *Reforming Welfare*.

DAVID FRUM is the author of *Dead Right* and *What's Right* published by New
Republic Books. A contributing editor to the new Washington magazine, *The
Weekly Standard*, and a senior fellow of the Manhattan Institute, he is a regular
commentator for print and broadcast media. From 1992 to 1994, he wrote the law
column for *Forbes* magazine, before which he served as an editor on the *Wall Street
Journal*.

TIM HAMES is a leader writer and political analyst for *The Times*. Before that he
was a lecturer in politics at Christ Church, Oxford, specialising in American
Government and Modern British Politics. His publications include *A Conservative*

Revolution: The Reagan-Thatcher Decade in Perspective and *Governing America*. His most recent paper *Lessons from the Republicans* is published by the SMF.

MYRON MAGNET is Editor of *City Journal*, the Manhattan Institute's quarterly publication. His writing has spanned topics ranging from American society and social policy, to economics, corporate management and intellectual history. His books include *Dickens and the Social Order* and, most recently, *The Dream and the Nightmare: The Sixties Legacy to the Underclass*. He has written more than fifty articles for *Fortune* magazine and is widely published elsewhere.

JAMES MILLER is president and co-founder of the Wisconsin Policy Research Institute. He has served as a Deputy Commissioner for the State of New York, as Associate Professor of Urban Affairs at the City University of New York, and as Director of Poverty Research for the US Catholic Conference. He has also worked as a consultant on a range of political campaigns and is a regular contributor to print and broadcast media.

CHARLES MURRAY is the Bradley Fellow at the American Enterprise Institute. From 1981 to 1990 he was a fellow with the Manhattan Institute. From 1974 to 1981, he worked for the American Institute for Research (AIR). His books include: *Losing Ground: American Social Policy 1950-1980*, *In Pursuit: Of Happiness and Good Government* and *The Bell Curve: Intelligence and Class Structure in American Life* co-written with the late Richard J. Hernnstein. He has recently published *What it means to be a Libertarian: A Personal Interpretation*. A renowned commentator, he has published and lectured extensively.

ROBERT SKIDELSKY is Chairman of the SMF and its Centre for Post-Collectivist Studies. He is Professor of Political Economy at Warwick University and was made a life peer in 1991. He is the biographer of John Maynard Keynes and author of *The World after Communism*. A regular political commentator, his latest book, *Beyond the Welfare State*, is published by the SMF.

NICHOLAS TIMMINS has been Public Policy Editor of the *Financial Times* since 1996, covering areas ranging from labour relations to social security. Previously he spent ten years on the *Independent*, first as Health and Social Services Correspondent, and later as Public Policy Editor. Before that he held similar posts at *The Times*. He is a visiting fellow at the Policy Studies Institute and author of *The Five Giants: A Biography of the Welfare State*.

DAVID WILLETTS is MP for Havant. A former adviser to the Downing Street Policy Unit on economic policy, health and social security, between 1986 and 1992 he was Director of Studies at the Centre for Policy Studies. He has occupied junior Ministerial posts and served as Paymaster-General in the Treasury. The former Chairman of Conservative Research Department, he is also a member of the SMF's Advisory Council. His books include *Civic Conservatism*, *Blair's Gurus* and *Is Conservatism Dead?* co-written with John Gray.

Foreword

Reforming welfare – how it is delivered, at whom it is targeted, who pays for it – has become one of the greatest public policy challenges facing post-industrial societies as they move towards the millennium.

In Britain, that task has been lent added urgency in the aftermath of Labour's election victory by a prime minister determined to make welfare reform a symbol of what it is about New Labour that is 'new'. As the following contributions make clear, and as the government has already discovered, genuine attempts at reform are fraught with difficulties both technical and political. They involve changing the intellectual climate and the mood of public opinion every bit as much as they require public policy innovation.

In these respects, Britain lags well behind the United States with its time limits on state assistance and work requirements for lone parents. A decentralised political system has also encouraged experimentation, such as using private agencies to get people off welfare into work and then paying these firms by results. The spur to that leadership position was a system which wasted so much public money and so many lives that 'thinking the unthinkable' became a necessity rather than a luxury.

How far Britain is willing and able to follow America

down the path of welfare reform before it is forced to do so by comparable levels of social breakdown is one of the major questions raised by this book. Amid the talk about hard choices, the definitive words on reforming welfare belong to Charles Murray – whose radical approach to poverty and welfare was pilloried in the 1980s but whose work went on to inspire many of the policies operating in the United States today. He says simply, 'this will hurt'.

Roderick Nye
February 1998

Chapter 1:
Myron Magnet

Why do men do what they do? Ask a policy analyst, and he is likely to depict not a human being but an economic calculating machine, totting up the worth of this benefit against that cost with the suave efficiency of a computer. But what drives actual men and women is not primarily the mechanical weighing of economic incentives, but a welter of fuzzier, harder-to-grasp realities. Chief among them are the impulses that come to us from culture, in other words from our beliefs and values. How much do we do out of a sense of honour, of duty, and also perhaps out of a wish to be cool or a fear of humiliation?

Every cultural moment has its own ideals, expressed in such embodiments as the great equestrian statue of Colleoni in Venice, not just the man but even his horse bristling from every pore with Renaissance confidence. Even that ideal figure of the policy experts, *homo economicus*, is an invention not of nature but of culture, distilled by Adam Smith from a rich mash of Calvinism and eighteenth-century Scottish rationalism. So what are we to make of that representative figure of American and also British urban culture – the unmarried welfare mother in a housing estate, with a school-dropout son who deals drugs and a daughter who is pregnant at fourteen?

Today's underclass, not only in America but also in Britain, is the product above all of culture not economics. I have argued this case before but I would like to summarise it briefly here. I will then go on to examine how the culture is changing right now – and how it is not changing – and what this means for the future of the underclass.

The big mystery about the underclass – the sub-group of

the poor whose high rates of non-work, school-leaving, illegitimacy, criminality, drug use and welfare dependency keep them in poverty even when economic opportunity proliferates around them – is this: why did it come into existence in America just when it shouldn't have? Back then, in the mid-1960s, the economy was strong, unemployment was low, and racial discrimination both in law and custom was beginning to crumble. Yet at that seemingly auspicious time the poor dropped out of school and out of the labour force at unprecedented rates, crime sky-rocketed, inner-city drug use grew phenomenally, and the urban poor crowded onto the rolls of welfare programmes that had been in existence since the 1930s but had until then never attracted such hordes of applicants. Why was this?

The answer is that at that moment the culture changed radically. The change began with the élite but inexorably trickled down from the universities, the media, the great philanthropic foundations, through the schools, the courts, the social workers and ultimately to the inner city. This change in basic beliefs and ideals, so great as to amount to a revolution, accomplished two distinct, if often mutually reinforcing, types of liberation. The first was personal – people did not want to be organisation men in grey flannel suits any more. They were sick of bourgeois morality, bourgeois culture and bourgeois respectability. They sought self-realisation and self-expression. They craved authenticity and fulfilment, not conformity.

The great expressions of this change were the sexual revolution and the counterculture. No, most people did not throw down their briefcases, braid flowers into their hair and join communes. But they came to think that their personal fulfilment – and especially their sexual fulfilment – was important enough to break up their marriages, as the huge increase in the divorce rate of that period attests (a rate which incidentally is not that much lower today). If people did not actually embrace ideas like dropping out, questioning authority and seeking altered states of consciousness in preference to mere rationality, at least they were happy to flirt with them. Drug use acquired a certain glamour, experimentation in everything from music to mushrooms, from bell bottoms to bedmates carried the day, and in direct proportion time-honoured forms of behaviour toward others lost their authority. Established virtues came to seem antique superstition. As Norman Mailer put it back then – when he was young and seemed full of promise – one was to 'forget the single mate, the solid family, the respectable love life' and 'follow the rebellious imperative of the self'.

Along with all this came a second liberation; political rather than personal, serious rather than frivolous. As the 1960s dawned America still bore the stain of official racism, and one of the praiseworthy accomplishments of that period was the sweeping success of the civil rights movement. The political part of the cultural revolution of the time sought to liberate the black and the poor from their marginalisation. But if the intention was noble, some of the consequences were quite the reverse.

The élite culture imagined that to accomplish this liberation, the poor and the black needed to be liberated from Western culture's bedrock traditional value: personal responsibility. No one phrased it quite that way at the time, but that was the whole tendency of this part of the cultural revolution. According to the new spirit of the age, the poor and the black were *ipso facto* victims; their condition was not the result of their own choices and actions but of vast, impersonal social and economic forces beyond their control. Racism denied them opportunity. And, according to the Marxoid ideas that were perhaps even more powerful among the British élite than the American, the same economic forces that were enriching the well-to-do were imprisoning the poor in their poverty. Vigorous capitalism required structural unemployment, a class of permanent victims. The poor were not responsible for their fate. Moreover, filled by their poverty with a sense of futility, they would not be able to seize the opportunity if it were available.

Thus, went the new orthodoxy, they needed reparations for the violence done them. If the systems we devised for our own profit were taking the bread out of their mouths, we owed them a living: we owed them welfare payments. This was not charity but simple justice.

If this class of victim committed crimes, again, they were not personally responsible. The system was to blame, not the criminal. Had not the system created a brutalising environment that bred crime in denying opportunity to some while the rest of the nation luxuriated in prosperity? Wasn't crime a kind of manly rebellion against that environment? Must we take care not to 'blame the victim', in the mantra of that period, which designated the mugger rather then the mugged as the real victim? In response, judges stripped away the order-keeping and crime-solving authority of the police, and treated accused criminals with increasing leniency. More important, by undermining the bedrock cultural understanding that crime is always wrong, the exculpatory idea of the criminal as victim subverted the prohibitions against crime in the consciences of individual criminals – and it is this set of cultural prohibitions, of thou-shalt-nots, that is after all the strongest bulwark against crime, far stronger than police and prisons. No wonder the crime rate soared out of sight from the mid-1960s onward.

It is important to remember that these new ideas were invested with powerful emotion. To many Americans, the goal of doing justice to the poor and the black was the highest, noblest good they could imagine, and the means of achieving that end likewise glowed with a halo of righteousness. So as proof of failure began to mount, many could not believe the evidence of their own senses. Surely an excess of these responsibility-sapping measures could not be the reason for growing welfare dependency, crime and the like. Instead, went the thinking, we must be doing too little and should do more.

But it was not only altruism that gave people such an emotional attachment to these ideas. The two liberations that made up the cultural revolution were closely intertwined with one another, and the righteousness of the political liberation seemed to many to infuse the personal liberation too. Were these not all part of a single great step forward in human freedom? The consequence was that self-gratification and self-indulgence could be seen as something more than mere selfishness – as something positive, almost philanthropic, rather like freeing the slaves. Indeed, if one made the condition of the worst-off the moral touchstone of society, as philosopher John Rawls famously did, one could feel justified in rejecting all its prohibitions as illegitimate, as long as one could impeach its treatment of the poor. So 'compassion' for the poor absolved one of a burden of personal responsibility of one's own.

How did these two creeds of liberation come together to form the underclass? Imagine how the new orthodoxy sounded from the vantage point of the inner city. For three decades, people had avoided going on benefit because of the shame attached to it. Suddenly it lost its stigma: the official culture's spokesmen – those whose voices were most prestigious and authoritative – were declaring loudly that welfare was no more than one's due for a wider economic plight that wasn't one's own responsibility. One was entitled to it, and indeed to take a low paid job instead would only be to conspire in one's own oppression. At the same time, top people, from the then attorney general to judges on the bench to newspaper editorialists, were saying that crime was not the criminal's responsibility. Potential criminals saw that Harvard professors, journalists and rock stars were celebrating the mind-expanding experience of drugs, and, while college kids experimented with marijuana and LSD, heroin and later cocaine enslaved the inner cities. In their rush for their own sexual liberation, the representatives of the élite culture removed the stigma from promiscuity, divorce and illegitimacy. Inner-city dwellers took the cue, and marriage in their neighbourhoods became a relic of the past. Children were brought up in non–families, too fragile to give them the nurture they needed to grow up and succeed. If most middle class people who had a fling with new culture ultimately landed on their feet, those at the bottom of society mostly did not.

The overarching message that the inner cities heard from the official culture was that you are absolved from responsibility and are not to blame. If the welfare state has an ideology, surely this is it. And ultimately, no more demoralising message can be given to anyone: you are not in control of your own life, it says, nothing is expected of you in the way of effort or conduct, you do not even rise to the level of moral – that is, individual human – significance. It is a message of deepest contempt, which fans the sense of aimlessness, meaninglessness and worthlessness of inner-city life. The welfare state is among other things a state of mind – a deeply nihilistic one, that sees man as only the sum of his material needs: *homo economicus* indeed.

These cultural changes began thirty years ago and more. Where are we today? And further, judging from today's trends, what can we foresee about the future of that demoralised underclass that is at once the great beneficiary of and the great reproach to the modern welfare state?

One set of trends is deeply hopeful. Almost four years ago, the citizens of New York, America's most liberal city, elected a mayor who built his campaign upon an approach to crime diametrically opposed to the orthodoxy of exculpation. That they could have elected a man so at odds with the prevailing outlook is evidence that they had begun to lose faith in it. This was hardly surprising since their city had turned into the murder capital of the world. Mayor Giuliani began to treat criminals as bad guys, not victims (based in part on theories he learnt at the Manhattan Institute). He arrested people who were disorderly in public spaces; he sent police out to patrol the streets aggressively, making it clear that the first duty of government is to protect the law-abiding from the lawless; and he publicly excoriated judges who released obvious malefactors on tortured technicalities. Lo and behold, the crime rate fell by over a third and the murder rate dropped by half, almost overnight, it now seems. New Yorkers had proof of what they had begun to suspect – treating criminals like victims creates anarchy. Sooner or later, reality has a way of disproving foolish ideas, however widely accepted or written into policy they are.

Similarly, last year we achieved national welfare reform, reflecting an important shift in American attitudes. The new reform declares an end to the welfare entitlement: you are no longer qualified to receive welfare simply by falling under a given income level, and once a state has agreed to pay you benefits, you can only receive them for a total of five years during your lifetime. This is a momentous change in fundamental assumptions, which commentators have not yet fully grasped.

For now the focus of welfare reform is on the requirement that recipients work for their benefits. This change satisfies both the followers of Charles Murray, who believe it will change the incentive structure and so change behaviour, and also cultural conservatives like myself, because, more important, it changes the message that the dominant culture gives to the poor. More often than not, people will do what the surrounding culture tells them is right. Yet it is also already clear that the Workfare programme is not the whole answer. In Milwaukee, Wisconsin – the other great Workfare success story, along with New York City – even as the welfare rolls drop, the illegitimacy rate, already America's highest, continues to rise. So further cultural changes are required.

A spate of new books and articles in America suggest that at long last the 1960s are finally over, and a new cultural era is under way. I think it is premature to say so. Despite the important examples just mentioned, you can list a host of counter-examples showing that the cultural revolution is still going full blast in the institutions of élite culture – and beyond. So today a titanic struggle for the culture is taking place, and it is not yet certain whether the underclass will get the message it needs to escape its self-defeating worldview and way of life.

The most visible current avatar of the cultural revolution is multiculturalism. Multiculturalism makes explicit the charge that the new culture only hinted at twenty-five or thirty years ago: that the entire structure of traditional Western values is aimed at oppressing the poor and non-white, and must therefore be 'deconstructed' – that is, trashed – in order to accomplish the liberation of the oppressed. These groups govern their lives according to their own values, equal and even superior to the traditional majority values of their oppressors. Now of course the underclass take pride of place among the oppressed, so they are at the very centre of the culture war today, fraught with momentous, if disputed, cultural significance.

What practical effect do such ideas have? To take one of the many recent examples of multiculturalism's influence: a judge in the Bronx recently dismissed a child abuse case against a mother who was beating and starving her toddler to drive out the devil that, she asserted, had taken possession of the child. To consider such behaviour criminal, ruled the sensitively multicultural judge, was not to understand the culture of the Bronx. Only slightly less extraterrestrial is the assertion of the flourishing Critical Race Theory school of law professors that the black community ought to embrace black lawbreaking as proper resistance to white oppression.

In fact, traditional Western culture turns out to be the wisdom distilled from three millennia of thought and experience about what life is the best for man, what can best realise his potentialities and give him a life that is meaningful and free. Only if the élite culture gives clear messages to the underclass that accord with these truths will the situation improve; the Back to Basics campaign failed in Britain because government ministers showed quite flamboyantly by their actions that they did not take seriously the family values they advocated. More honest at least, if no less corrosive, was the well-known London television and newspaper commentator who, after listening to the argument that her own conduct ought to be an example to the worse-off, slapped her hand on the table and cried: 'I don't care! I'm not giving up my liberation!'

I would like to finish with a vignette that sums up the cultural moment right now. It happens to be set in England. The Dean of Winchester some months ago invited the youth of the area to a 'rave' in his cathedral. At the rave the dancers aimed to work themselves up into a sort of Dionysian frenzy by means of loud, pulsating music, ceaseless gyrating on the dance floor, and liberal use of angel dust or PCP. They came to the cathedral, over a thousand strong; they had their music, they took their drugs and they danced their frenzied dance literally on Jane Austen's grave. This is a perfect emblem of the culture we do not want – and its consequences.

Chapter 2:
Robert Skidelsky

Myron Magnet has argued that the causes of the dependency culture are largely cultural. He has outlined a number of cultural causes. These are not confined to the United States. We have had them in this country. We could talk about them in very much the same way. For example, we could talk about the breakdown of Victorian values or the hedonistic culture of the 1960s as causes of the decline of individual responsibility; we could also talk about 'a culture of victimhood'.

There is also the political critique of capitalism, the idea that it was the system and not individuals that was responsible for their misfortunes. Therefore, society had a duty to do something about it.

This welfare imperative went a long way beyond the acceptance of the traditional duty of the state to look after those who genuinely could not take care of themselves. It extended to people able to work and provide for themselves in the normal way. There were no specific disabilities attached to them, except their membership to a system that was itself unjust. This kind of critique also extended to the institutions of that society, not just the economic institutions, but cultural institutions like the patriarchal family.

Norman Dennis, who has criticised the welfare state from the point of view of an ethical socialist, has argued that the destabilisation of the traditional family was brought about by a quasi-Marxist intelligensia. Again, this would be one kind of cultural analysis of the social pathologies of our time.

A third kind of analysis draws attention to the role of what Howard Glennerster calls 'social policy based pressure groups'– the welfare advocates. The organised, providing professions – like doctors, teachers, unions and local officials – became lobbies for greater spending with close ties to spending departments. Spending departments set up expert committees which identified areas of need and called for the meeting of need with increased expenditure. The welfare lobbies were crucial not only in extending the range of entitlements but also informing people of their rights.

Gradually new classes of victims were created as gaps in existing provisions were identified and people were encouraged to claim the benefits that were made available. One of the features of the expansion of the welfare state, which became very pronounced from the 1960s onwards, was not only that the range of entitlements was extended, but that the take-up of entitlements increased over time. This is not just because people became better informed of their rights. People also changed their behaviour in order to qualify for the benefits that were being offered. The crucial shift in the 1960s in public discussions of the functions of the welfare state was the invention of the concept of relative poverty.

When our welfare state was set up poverty was defined in absolute terms as falling below the ability to command a bundle of necessities, which was defined in physical terms: quantities of food, quantities of clothing, housing, and so on. The relief of poverty therefore became simply the provision of this subsistence. By the 1960s this was thought to be an inadequate description of what poverty was. It was defined in relation not to absolute subsistence needs but to the national income – more specifically it came to be defined as having less than a certain share of the national income, usually half.

This has had two consequences. First, it means that the poor are always with us. Second, it means that any programme to relieve poverty is *ipso facto* a programme for minimising income inequalities. In other words, the provision of welfare became firmly hitched to the traditional socialist programme, which was precisely to minimise income inequalities and create greater equality of outcome.

It is at this point that I believe the welfare state started to lose some of its legitimacy. The point at which criticisms of the welfare state started to become more persistent coincides with this shift in its function from the relief of absolute poverty to the state's duty to minimise income inequalities. This, of course, entailed a very much larger redistributive role for the state than had been implicit in the founding ideas of the welfare state.

It could be said that this is a cultural shift, a shift in people's ways of thinking about poverty, as well as a change in general cultural attitudes. Economics has something to say about this. What you find in this discussion are really two literatures which have very few points of contact. There is the economics literature, which talks about the unaffordability of the welfare state, its effect on public finances, its possible effects on economic growth, on the incentives facing people in the job market and so on. Then there is the cultural literature about dependency, character and victimhood.

I do not believe the economics literature is negligible. The reason why there is so much debate about the future of welfare is because most people believe that the welfare state, in its present form, is unaffordable. Taxpayers are not prepared to pay its cost. Therefore, it will have to be slimmed down. You can challenge this view, but it is an almost universal assumption. It is an assumption shared by the new Labour government as well as the previous Conservative government. It means one of two things. Either the welfare state will have to be slimmed down absolutely; that is to say, the government will have to spend less on welfare which means that if we want the existing services to continue to be supplied, people will have to spend more of their own money on them. This is one implication. The second is, I believe, one which the Labour government has in mind. This is to redirect cash transfers from the poor to the services which people care most about; from social security to the National Health Service and education. 'Reform', I believe, means a redirection of spending, rather than a cut in absolute spending.

I know that Frank Field, from his published writings, accepts a large part of the cultural critique discussed by Myron Magnet, and emphasises the effect of the welfare state on character, on its reduction in the sense of individual responsibility, and on setting up a perverse kind of game which encourages people to behave badly rather than well. This is where I believe the economist has something to say. Of course, the economist's view is inadequate. Indeed, the economist views culture largely as a function of the incentives set up in any given society. The premise is that people are rational and they will take what they can get. If you set up a game in which, for example, you reward single parenthood above married life, you will get an increase in single parents. If you have a criminal justice system which either does not catch people when they commit crimes, or which lowers the cost of committing crimes, you will have more crime. It is as simple as that. You do not need to bring culture into your explanation.

I found it useful, in trying to think through this subject, to develop an economic concept which throws light on the cultural aspects we have been dealing with. To describe it, I have used the phrase 'moral hazard'. In some ways it is an unfortunate term, because it suggests that the people who are on benefits, who exploit the welfare state, are behaving immorally and therefore ought to be blamed for their behaviour. It carries this connotation of blame whereas in fact, it is quite a neutral concept and is used simply to describe a situation where a person can maximise his or her satisfaction at the expense of others; that is, can make others pay for the consequences of self-interested behaviour. It does not apply solely to the lowest income groups, the poorest in society, but operates at all levels of society. A mother, and I am using an English example here, who drops out of work so that her child can qualify for an assisted place at an independent school, is exploiting the system, just as much as the unmarried mother who has babies on the state.

I am really talking about manipulable contingencies: this is the essence of moral hazard. You can see how the welfare state can actually create the victims it needs to support by simply defining as eligible for benefit people who find themselves in a particular situation which they can create for themselves. Of course there are some contingencies you have no control over, for example, growing old. Having children, however, is a contingency you do have control over. You have a certain amount of control over whether you are employed or unemployed, though forces of nature can influence that too, like a great depression.

Society is full of examples like these where people have some control over what position they are in. If you set up a system of entitlements for manipulable contingencies the state will acquire almost unlimited liabilities in the end. I believe this, to some extent, has already happened.

You cannot say such behaviour is irrational. In fact it is highly rational. Beveridge, the founder of the British welfare state, once said that it was a person's duty to claim the dole if he could get more out of it than by working. 'Duty' is surely the wrong word. It is not a person's duty to claim the dole if he or she can get more from it than by working, but it is perfectly rational to do so.

If you set up a system in which it is rational for people to inflict costs on third parties for their own behaviour, then you will get an increase in third party costs. You cannot just say that this is a non-problem. The expectation in 1944 and after, when the British welfare state was set up, was that it would be a shrinking proportion of national income; that poverty would decrease as societies became more prosperous; and that if you had full employment you would not need to use the welfare system nearly as much. Full employment was seen as the cheapest form of welfare. It cost nothing and made recourse to benefits much less likely.

Instead, what happened was continual expansion. The number of people claiming benefits rose and rose and rose.

For one category – the means-tested benefits – 800,000 claimed them in 1948; by 1995 the figure had risen to 9 million. You might say this is due to the deterioration in economic conditions in the 1980s and the subsequent rise in unemployment and the collateral damage of unemployment. Of course it is partly due to this. But this rise started when we were at full employment, when we were in the Golden Age. The rise started at the end of the 1940s and, by 1966, there were already nearly 3 million claimants. (I am using the two figures slightly differently; there were 3 million claimants, which means there were many more recipients – even in the mid-1960s.)

This rise is not all because of what has happened since the economic slowdown. There is a connection between the economic slowdown and the increase of the welfare state, but what is it? It is a very complicated question. I have my own ideas of how one should set about reform, though I have no pat solution to some of the more intractable problems like the breakdown of the family. On pensions it seems reasonably easy. Conceptually it *is* quite easy. Politically and administratively it is not so easy because of the problem of double payment. You simply have to convert the present pay-as-you-go scheme into a properly funded scheme. That is to say, pensions provision should be based on a system of compulsory saving. This would give you a much better deal, per pensioner, in the long run than the present National Insurance system, which is a pay-as-you-go system and does not lead to any increase through investment of your entitlement over time. In fact there is no relation whatever between what you pay in and what you get. Both are politically determined and they are simply a function of current politics, such as they are.

Pension reform along these lines will happen. There is no doubt about it. Peter Lilley started the process. The Labour Party attacked it for political reasons, but in fact Peter Lilley got much of the idea from Frank Field in the first place. So there is going to be all-party support for reform along these lines.

Other kinds of insurance can also be made proper insurance. You can have a proper unemployment insurance fund, provided government is able to maintain some degree of economic stabilisation. The government should do the things in which it has a comparative advantage, and keep out of things it does badly. One of the things it can do, if it conducts its macro-policy properly, is to maintain a reasonably stable high level of employment. If it succeeds then it will be able to run an unemployment insurance scheme on an actuarial basis. Such schemes have run for many periods in this century. The original unemployment insurance fund only collapsed in the great depression of the early 1930s. So in that area it is quite easy to see how we can make some progress.

Regarding the long-term unemployed, I support the idea of giving them an offer of either a job or training. If they do not take either then their benefit rights are severely curtailed. This was started in a small way by the previous government. The Labour government intends to make a much larger splash. They intend it to cover more people and I believe it will do good. The trouble with all these schemes is that if they are badly done they do not do any good. They simply produce dead-end jobs. If they are well done, however – with a bit of panache – they could be a very important way for people to recover their self-respect and become employable in what you might call permanent jobs again. They may also have a beneficial side effect, which is to make young unemployed working-class men more marriageable again, more eligible as partners, and may therefore do something to cap the explosion of single parent families.

The most difficult problem of all is to wean people off the means-tested benefits. What we have done in this country since the 1960s is to set up a vast system of Speenhamland. That is, the system of wage subsidies, which gets its name from the County of Berkshire in 1795 when, in a period of high inflation, the local rates started to subsidise the wages of agricultural labourers. The system of in-work benefits is simply a modern version of that old poor law system, which was abolished by the new poor law of 1834.

I do not consider this is a good system. My basic principle is that the poor in work should be taken out of the benefit system. If we want to relieve their poverty this should be done by relieving them of tax, or giving them tax credits, not by attaching them to the benefit administration.

We need to reform the system not just because it is unaffordable or because it may have adverse cultural consequences. We need to reform it because I do not believe that the welfare state, such as we now have, does anything for the spirit of liberty. Liberty is something which is of supreme value. You have got to give people the right and the ability to choose their patterns of life. In order to do that they have got to have much more spending power in making those choices than the state now leaves them. I base my arguments for reform on the idea that if you want a free society you cannot have the state spending as much as it does now. My reforms are ultimately designed to bring about lower taxes and to give earners more freedom to provide for their welfare needs themselves.

Chapter 3:
David Willetts

There are two very different ways of looking at the welfare problem. One approach focuses on the cost of the nearly £100 billion of social security spending every year. It worries about the inefficiency of the system and the complicated ways in which benefits interact with each other and with the tax system. The aim is to find a simpler, cheaper system. It eschews value judgements and focuses on technocratic solutions. Tax-benefit integration, for which Tony Blair has given Martin Taylor personal responsibility, is the biggest and boldest of the technocratic solutions on offer.

There is also a second rather different approach. This focuses on the effects of the welfare system on behaviour. The problem is seen as not just how much it costs but what it does to the people who depend on it. Frank Field is a leading critic from this school, eloquently warning of the morally corrosive effects of means-tests. He wants to move away from means-tests and towards universal benefits which are based on the morally elevated contributory principle, rather than what he sees as the morally devalued tradition of income support, supplementary benefit, national assistance, the Poor Law. He truly wants to take us back to Beveridge.

It is a revealing example of Tony Blair's style of government that he appears to have endorsed both approaches. On the one hand Martin Taylor is to work for Gordon Brown on the ultimate technocratic solution, the biggest and best means-test of the lot delivered by integrating tax and benefits. On the other hand Frank Field is pursuing his moral vision of the reformed welfare system with genuine personal contributions. It is just like the

Brighouse Woodhead approach to education reform. My first warning is that welfare reform will go nowhere unless the Treasury and the Department of Social Security are in some sort of harmony. Martin Taylor needs to thrash this out with Frank Field early on.

How to increase marginal rates by cutting them

The tax and social security problem which we hear about most is the high marginal rates of taxation and the withdrawal of benefits. Here you are wrestling with the laws of arithmetic.

In particular I advise not, paradoxically, to increase marginal rates by cutting them. Let us look at an example. Imagine that a family is receiving £100 a week of Income Support with no other income – these are schematic figures. You have in effect set a minimum income of £100 a week. Then you take away that benefit pound for pound, so for every £1 you earn up to £100, you lose £1 of benefit and are no better off. But after your earnings get above £100 you are then out of the system. At that point every £1 you earn extra you keep. This is very schematic but it reveals the basic arithmetical point.

Then someone comes along and says that it is absurd for someone who is earning £50 to be caught in a 100 per cent marginal rate. What we should have is a system in which for every pound you earn from the very first pound you keep, say, 50 per cent of it. The tax and benefit system is revised so that instead of facing a 100 per cent rate of tax and benefit withdrawal you now face 50 per cent tax-benefit withdrawal.

This is fine so far but two consequences follow. The first is that you have increased the incomes not just of people earning £100 but those earning over £100 as well. The system is still tapering out. You are going to have a higher net income because you are keeping some of your benefits and you are earning £100. That higher net income is either higher social security expenditure or it is lower tax receipts but it has a PSBR cost. This is the first consequence.

The second is that the combined marginal tax rate and benefit withdrawal rate of someone earning between £100 and £200 a week has now been increased. They are now losing benefits at a 50 per cent rate, whereas before they were out of this trap. If you have a concentration of people in the labour market within this range of earnings, it is a high price to pay – dealing with the admitted anomaly at the bottom of the earnings scale.

My advice on marginal rates is as follows. Nobody who tells you he is going to reduce the marginal rate to 90 per cent or 70 per cent or whatever, should be allowed to get away with it unless he also tells you two things. First, how much is it going to cost and second, how many people higher up the earnings scale are going to find themselves brought into the system and paying a higher marginal rate than they did before?

Whatever happened to our earned income tax credit?

We are told that Gordon Brown is keen to copy the American Earned Income Tax Credit. When I was in the Policy Unit during Norman Fowler's Social Security Review, I was similarly excited by this American example. It is a personal tax allowance which is withdrawn as you move higher up the income scale – if you like, a targeted personal allowance. It has its drawbacks however, such as the higher marginal rate for those people who are having the tax allowance withdrawn. The Green Paper that we produced in 1985 as part of Norman Fowler's Social Security Reform advocated a tax credit to be payable to all low income families, withdrawn as their incomes rose. We ended up with the Family Credit, which many in the Labour Party rubbish, instead of the original Earned Income Tax Credit. It is a case study in the practical difficulties of tax-benefit integration.

If you want people to be better off in work than out of work, and you top up their work earnings to ensure that they are, then the structure of your in-work top-up has to mirror the structure of your out-of-work benefit: the benefits shape the credit. Once this has happened, there are strong practical arguments for using the benefit system to calculate the entitlements because you are doing a benefit-type enquiry, much more complicated than the income tax authorities would ever envisage.

Even though Family Credit entitlement was going to be calculated by the benefit authorities, Conservatives still hoped it would be delivered in the form of a tax credit to people in work, using PAYE. This was in our Bill, but it was defeated in the House of Lords by an alliance of two groups. The small business lobby complained that employers were going to be asked to carry out much more complicated calculations to deliver PAYE than they had in the past and they feared it would be an unfair burden on business. There was also a campaign (involving many people in the Labour Party) about 'wallet versus purse'. The critics wanted a family benefit to go into the purse of the mother who might well not be working, rather than in the wallet of the working father.

This is why we did not have the full American Earned Income Tax Credit when we tried ten years ago. We ended up with Family Credit, which tries to do exactly the things that the Earned Income Tax Credit does to boost the incomes of low-income working families. Incidentally, Family Credit is denounced by Labour on the grounds that it supposedly subsidises bad employers. If so, why don't Earned Income Tax Credits do the same?

Who? Whom? Don't hide behind technocratic devices

Lenin said in his ruthless way that the question to ask of any social institution was: 'Who? Whom?' i.e. what is the balance of interests? It is worth asking any person with a pet scheme for reforming social security who they wish to be better off as a result of these proposals and who they are trying to take the money from. What are the distributional impacts of their proposals? Anybody seriously approaching social security should do so with a view about what sort of distributional changes they wish to achieve. Too often, however, ingenious technocratic devices are used to disguise this fundamental question. One reads a book or pamphlet advocating some ingenious new system of social security, but it is not clear at the end exactly who is going to be better off and who is going to be worse off. Sometimes the technocrats defend their new systems by saying that they are so ingenious they can replicate the current distribution of income. In which case, why bother going through a massive turbulent change in order simply to replicate what the current system is doing?

Technocratic change is not an end in itself. It is only a device for achieving other ends. One of the most important ends that people should focus on is the view they take of the current impact of the tax and benefit system on income distribution and how they would like it to be different. Do not take a reformer seriously until he is willing to come clean on the one issue Labour used to talk about all the time: distribution.

Beware averages

Even if you do get some analysis of the distributional impact of your proposed changes, it might not tell the whole story. If your scheme helps some groups and if, say, 250,000 households lose £1 a week you might think it is manageable. But what if within those 250,000 there are 50,000 households losing substantially more? And what if that includes some people managing on very low incomes indeed? You may have to press the analysts hard to discover this but it is uncomfortable side-effects such as these which often make it difficult to pursue some grand vision of benefit reform.

This is also one of the reasons why welfare reform can so easily end up costing money. The gainers gain and the people at risk of losing are compensated. You will end up compromising by moving towards your objective incrementally, trying to protect people from cash losses. This slow and careful process is far removed from the dramatic 'big bang' solutions which the political masters may be after.

Tax-benefit integration

The Family Credit episode is but the latest example of a series of attempts at achieving that elusive goal of tax-benefit integration. It was a big plank of Harold Wilson's platform in 1964 and we could do a lot worse than study the Houghton/Crossman attempt at tax-benefit integration at that time. The grand schemes of the 1960s and 1970s betray the same sort of mentality as the ambitious town planners trying to reconstruct our cities.

Tax-benefit integration is an example of the egregious errors we have already identified. Its advocates fail to explain what is the distribution impact they wish to achieve by uprooting the system in this way. They present their schemes as dealing with the problem of high marginal rates but we need to know how many people higher up the income scale will have higher marginal rates as a result.

This is not the end of the story. Paying in is not the same as taking out. Paying taxes is not the same as receiving social security benefits. A merged new government Income

Adjustment Service would somehow suggest that being a net payer-in or a net receiver all boils down to the same thing. It fails to convey how we should approach our responsibilities as citizens. It is incompatible with Tony Blair's rhetoric of rights matched by duties because it muddles our right to benefit and our duty to pay tax.

What will be presented by others as tiresome administrative problems actually reflect these deeper cultural issues. An apparently obscure technical issue – the relevant period to be covered – reveals these deep issues. Tax is calculated on our incomes over a year. But if someone turns up destitute at a benefit office in November, the fact that they had an income in May is not relevant. Means-tested benefits cover much shorter periods.

Then there is the question of the family unit. We have moved towards independent taxation of husband and wife but is the non-working wife of a City banker to be entitled to Income Support? Of course not. If she gets a paid job, is her income then to be taxed independently of his? Of course it must. The benefits system deals with households whereas the tax system deals with individuals.

There is a sociological explanation of the fashionableness of tax-benefit integration. Most of the pundits, journalists and commentators who advocate integration probably fill in a complicated tax return rather than just relying on PAYE. Poor people deal with a benefit system which also feels complicated to them. There is detailed investigation of their income and they have to declare information about personal expenses. Many imagine that somehow the Income Support system dealing with people on low incomes and a tax system dealing with people with complicated tax affairs are doing the same type of thing. In which case, they ask, why do we not just merge these two Whitehall departments that are just asking the same kind of question but of two different groups? But there is not a continuum. In the middle, between those who are filling in tax returns and people on low incomes, there is a vast number of people whose dealings with the tax and benefits systems are relatively straightforward. They are on PAYE and not filling in a tax return. They may be in receipt of child benefit or a retirement pension, about which the state knows incredibly little – and quite rightly so. There is far less information about them than the Revenue needs for someone completing a tax return, and much less than the Income Support system needs.

There is no continuum along which we are all facing these intrusive and complicated questions. Virtually any system of tax–benefit integration will end up with a model in which you start asking all these people in the middle a large number of completely unnecessary questions. Far from making things simpler, such changes can actually make them more complicated.

Targeting and means-testing are not synonymous

Why have people invested so much effort in pursuing that elusive goal of tax-benefit integration? What drives it is the pursuit of the ideal means-test. Inevitably the tax system looks like the right model and attempts are then made to wrench the benefit system into a tax-like form – attempts which, as we saw above, encounter serious obstacles because of the failure to understand the cultural differences between taxes and benefits.

There is another misunderstanding behind the pursuit of this will-o'-the-wisp. We all believe that benefits need to be targeted to people who really need them. Targeting is thought to be synonymous with means-testing, and if you are looking for a good means-test the tax system seems to be your model. But means-testing is only one way of achieving the aim of targeting. It was Beveridge's crucial insight that if you define your categories of claimants carefully enough you can have a benefit which is pretty well-targeted without being means-tested.

This is why I have advocated focusing Child Benefit on children under five, for example. Poorest families are one-earner families and one-earner families tend to be families with pre-school children. (No-earner families are in practice helped by Income Support rather than Child Benefit.) Targeting need not, therefore, involve means-testing.

Why Beveridge's figures never added up

As tax-benefit integration faces such difficulties, is Frank Field's approach taking us back to Beveridge and a better way forward? The conventional view is that the Beveridge Report was a marvellous document, a great vision of the future, and the only trouble is that because society has changed Beveridge's model is no longer appropriate. We are told Beveridge's plan would have worked but for the high rate of unemployment we began to experience in the 1970s, or higher rates of marriage break-up and the rise of single-parent families.

This is largely irrelevant. Beveridge's model has internal contradictions that are completely independent of social change. If British society had remained unchanged after 1945, the Beveridge model would still have faced a fundamental difficulty. He fails to reconcile three objectives. First, he wants people to have contributory benefits, benefits received as a result of their National Insurance contributions, that float them off means-tested assistance. This requires a contributory benefit that is better than the old means-tested benefit and available to more people. Second, he does not want the National Insurance contributions to be so high that they impose an unsustainable burden on the working population. Third, he wants his National Insurance contributions to finance his National Insurance benefits. Beveridge is incapable in his own report of squaring that circle.

He avoids the challenge in two ways. First, he is extremely unclear as to whether he envisages that his contributory benefits could be of any greater value than the National Assistance which they are supposed to be replacing. And second, even at the end of twenty years of his scheme, he still envisaged almost half the costs being paid for by subsidies from the Treasury. The National Insurance contributions, set at a level that was acceptable and affordable for the working population, could not actually finance the level of benefits he was envisaging. So there were still significant transfers coming from the Treasury out of general taxation.

This is not just of historical interest. Frank Field, whom we all admire, is trapped in exactly the same dilemma. He is an eloquent and passionate critic of the effects of means-testing on behaviour. What is his solution? It is to shift from means-testing to universal contributory benefits. He cannot pretend that his universal system, which is intended to displace means-tested benefits, can possibly be cheaper than the current system. What he is talking about is floating people off means-tested benefits by having higher contributory benefits instead. He recognises this will mean a significant increase in the tax burden; some combination of higher National Insurance contributions and higher taxes to pay the contributions of people who are not able to pay their contributions themselves. It is the same as the Beveridge trap. It is the problem of delivering a contributory system in practice – to get people off means-tested benefits by giving them non-means-tested benefits can be very expensive indeed. Beveridge could never get his figures to add up and Frank Field won't either.

When is compulsory saving better than a tax?

If the sums of money we save are very small then the transaction costs can be relatively high. That is why Peter Lilley looked at, but rejected, the option of simply privatising the State Earnings Related Pension Scheme (SERPS) – the compulsory second pension. He concluded that the transaction costs were too high to make the game worth the candle, and that we would return to the same arguments we had about personal pensions. It is why Peter Lilley instead, quite rightly, went for the more radical option of offering young people entering the labour market the prospect of a personal pension fund that would not just replace SERPS but also replace the basic pension.

Frank Field talks about how he wants to see everybody having a personal pension fund too. Fine. But he is then going to find himself impaled on exactly the same dilemma the Conservatives faced whenever we looked at this in government. Simply doing it for SERPS is going to lead to high ratios of transaction costs to the value of the savings. It is only worthwhile if you also include the basic state pension, and once you include the basic state pension you are back to the very proposal which Tony Blair denounced in the last week of the election campaign. It will be interesting to watch Labour try to escape from this dilemma.

Contributions and means-tests: Taylor versus Field

The social security debate in this country has developed in two very different directions. One option is the bigger, better means-test. This is where the remit to work on tax-benefit integration comes in and I have tried to warn of the pitfalls which have defeated all previous attempts at achieving this. The second option aims to restore the contributory principle at the centre of social security – Frank Field's agenda. Here the aim is not to make social security like tax but to make it more like real saving and genuine insurance. Then there is supposed to be a morally elevated sense that benefits have been paid for. This option also has its difficulties: it involves escalating benefits and higher contributions. One thing is for sure: Tony Blair cannot move in both directions at the same time. At some point someone is going to have to make some hard decisions.

Chapter 4:
David Frum

It is, when you think about it, quite remarkable that we are debating the future of welfare. To all outward appearance, the political pendulum of the North Atlantic is swinging to the left. Last year, Bill Clinton won re-election as president of the United States: the first Democrat to do so since Harry Truman. In Canada, my homeland, the Liberal government is cruising to an easy re-election victory, which will be its first back-to-back parliamentary majority since 1953. And here in the United Kingdom, the Labour Party won the largest victory in its history.

So why are we considering giving less money to poor people? Why aren't we debating whether we should be taking more money away from rich people? Why are ideas once thoroughly repudiated - such as a work requirement for people on public assistance and the absolute cut-off of aid to the young and able-bodied — resurfacing now as serious proposals, and in some cases as actual law? And why are parties of the Left signing on to these ideas? Let me remind people of how Liberals, Democrats and the Labour Party once responded to criticism of welfare programmes. Hubert Humphrey, campaigning for president in 1976, declared that 'candidates who make an attack on welfare are making an attack on government programmes, on blacks, on minorities, on the cities. It's a disguised new form of racism, a disguised new form of conservatism.' It is a remark valuable for its absolutely pristine preservation of a vanished historical moment. It is like discovering an ancient Byzantine alabaster cup without even a chip in it. But it is not enough to treasure these antique words. We must study them.

In the run-up to the 1988 presidential election in the

United States, Jack Kemp warned Republicans against the vacuous campaign they were planning to run that year. 'We cannot', he said, 'count on our opponents to go on digging their own graves election after election.' He was wrong in 1988. The Democrats did dig their own grave one last time, nominating a short liberal from Brookline and featuring him in television ads sticking out of the top of a tank with a Snoopy hat on his head. But his wider point was right. For twenty-five years, Republicans in the United States and Tories in Britain have profited from the thraldom of the parties of the Left to the sort of ideology Humphrey was speaking for. In the United States it is called liberalism, I am not sure what it is called in Britain. In the late 1960s and early 1970s, this sort of liberalism became a stink in the nostrils of the middle class and lower middle class voters who elected Franklin Delano Roosevelt, the Democratic congresses of the 1950s; who in Britain supported tough Labour politicians like Clement Attlee and Hugh Gaitskell.

In the mid-1970s, Jonathan Rieder, a Yale sociologist, went to live for two years in the New York neighbourhood of Canarsie, a section of Brooklyn that lies to the south and west of Kennedy Airport. Canarsie, a heavily Jewish and Italian neighbourhood, had once been a bastion of the Democratic Party, but since the late 1960s it had shown itself increasingly willing to vote Republican. Rieder, a man of the Left, wanted to understand better why the people of Canarsie had taken to voting against what he perceived as their class interest. In his summary of what he found, he concluded:

Since 1960 the Jews and Italians of Canarsie have embellished and modified the meaning of liberalism, associating it with profligacy, spinelessness, malevolence, masochism, élitism, fantasy, anarchy, idealism, softness, irresponsibility and sanctimony. The term conservative acquired connotations of pragmatism, character, reciprocity, truthfulness, stoicism, manliness, realism, hardness, vengeance, strictness, and responsibility.

What Bill Clinton and Tony Blair both understand is that much of the bad odour that has clung to their parties originates in their attitudes to welfare. Why welfare? After all, welfare (strictly defined) is a tiny programme in the United States and costs about one per cent of the federal budget, or $15 billion, and costs state and local governments about the same. Let me offer three explanations for the huge increase in the United States.

First is the link between welfare and crime. Polls routinely ask Americans what they regard as the country's most important issue. If you look back over the past twenty-five years worth of polls, when the country is prosperous and at peace, the answer is almost always the same: crime or drugs, a synonym for crime. When the economy is in recession, crime usually ranks second after jobs. Crime rates and long-term welfare dependency both began to rise in the United States at the same time, in the early and mid-1960s. Policy makers can debate the relationship between the two. Did one cause the other? Was there some third cause that drove both? Was demography at work? Changing conditions in the labour market? Plain coincidence? But working Americans do not bother with sophisticated analysis. They believe the two are linked, and that where there is a welfare population – black or white – there is crime. I imagine Britons believe the same. And, in America, people quickly suspected that their leaders, no matter what else they might say, also perceived some sort of link. Why else was it that the politicians most keenly in favour of more generous welfare benefits were also the politicians most hostile to the police and least eager to lengthen jail sentences and hasten the conviction of criminals? By the 1990s, I believe, welfare and crime were seen as one issue in the American mind; the issue of the urban underclass – what to do about it and how to protect everybody else from it.

The second fact that drives the welfare debate, it seems to me, is the implicit link between this issue and the issues of work and success. Politicians on the Left used to say – and I suspect they still believe this, no matter what else they say – that success in our society (in those more candid days, a British politician of the Left would have said, 'in a non-socialist society') was distributed with almost perfect randomness. What greater figure of fun was there than the self-made man, boasting of how he owed everything to hard work? The Monty Python team alone made half a dozen sketches out of him.

A practical politician in those days might understand that bringing socialism to the United States, or even Britain, was not feasible. But what he would also think is that, in the absence of socialism, the least life's winners could do for life's losers was slice them a piece of their income and hand it over. In Britain it would be called redistribution, in America it is called fairness and behind it lies the belief that is almost never true that success or failure in life is morally laudable or blameworthy.

To life's big winners that argument might sound halfway plausible. The rich men I know all readily concede that they lived through one, two or half a dozen crises when, with a bit of bad luck, they could have lost everything they had. And the members of what Charles Murray has called the 'cognitive élite' – society's talkers and thinkers and planners – likewise, I think, sense that while they may owe their success in life to their cleverness, they owe their cleverness to a lucky draw in the dealing out of genetic cards.

But life's smaller winners do not see things that way, and this is why liberalism of the American sort – or the British version of it packaged by the *Guardian* – so deeply offends them. The difference between a man who ekes out a living from a news stand and the man who never holds a steady job, between a woman who dresses her children and sends them to school with her earnings from house cleaning and the woman who lives on welfare, is not the same as the difference between the lucky and the unlucky commodities speculator or the child born clever and the child born slow. This is a matter of character; to the people involved it seems to be a moral difference, and policies that tend to equalise the economic rewards of the news vendor and the layabout are offending against the moral code by which most Americans, and, I suspect, most British, still live.

The third and last of these welfare issues is the hardest to put one's finger on and yet also the most important. One of the most famous observations by Thomas Jefferson is his remark, in *Notes on the State of Virginia*, that, 'Those who labour in the earth are the chosen people of God.' But it is worth remembering why Jefferson thought so highly of farmers and looked down on city dwellers. Farmers, he believed, relied on their own industry more than any other class of society. Industrial workers and city dwellers generally depended on what he called 'the casualties and caprice' of others. And then he warned, 'Dependence begets subservience and venality, suffocates the germ of virtue and prepares fit tools for the design of ambition.' In his mind, the collapse of the ancient republics of Greece and Rome was directly connected to the growth of great cities full of people who relied for their subsistence on the benevolence of others:

> The mobs of great cities add just so much to the support
> of pure government as sores do to the strength of the
> human body. It is the manners and spirit of a people
> which preserve a republic in vigour. A degeneracy in
> these is a canker which soon eats to the heart of its laws
> and constitution.

I do not quote these words to endorse them. Obviously anyone who regarded the farmer as uniquely self-reliant was born before the era of agricultural subsidies. But the anxieties that Jefferson expresses, I believe, are held in less eloquent form by almost every American: someone who depends for his livelihood not on his own efforts but on the goodwill or charity of someone else cannot be a full citizen, and the presence of large numbers of permanently dependent people poses a threat to the vitality and strength of a republic. The urban underclass in America dismays people precisely because it seems un-American, because the existence of some 3 million people, clustered for the most part at the very centre of America's greatest cities, who live for years, even decades at a stretch, on the charity of government and whose children live in the same way after them, offends some primordial self-understanding of the American nation. How often does a congressman hear the angry voice of the voter shouting at him on his telephone, 'I have my rights! I'm a taxpayer!' The two go hand in hand in the popular mind. And since it would be even more un-American to suggest that people on welfare do not have rights, it is then their status as dependants, not taxpayers, that baffles and discomfits their fellow citizens.

As I mentioned earlier, Bill Clinton and Tony Blair successfully grasped the meaning of these truths about welfare for parties of the Left: whatever a party of the Left actually does, it must above all appear to cherish work above welfare, indeed to insist on work for everyone. Each of them has a variety of incredibly elaborate schemes to move people from welfare to work without unduly upsetting the immense network of social workers, administrators and activists who voted for them. I leave it to others to question whether these schemes can work. I only note that the salesmen of ersatz products – leatherette, diet Coke, knock-off watches – always promise that their goods are indistinguishable from the real thing and always disappoint their customers. The same is probably true of ersatz work and ersatz responsibility.

Instead, I will look at something else. How should parties of the Right deal with the politics of welfare now that the parties of the Left have taken Jack Kemp's advice and stopped committing electoral suicide? The very first thing they must do, it should go without saying, is not relax. They should carefully monitor welfare reforms and be ready to call the public's attention when the cause of reform is hijacked. Real reforms, like those in the state of Wisconsin, do not permit people to use training courses indefinitely to postpone work, are not easily persuaded that someone is incapable of work, and measure their success by their ability to move people to productive jobs in the private sector. In the United States, this will principally be an issue at the state level; in Britain it will be one of the most important tasks facing the Tory Party in opposition.

In America, conservatives face a second and related problem. Governments have long resented the vitality and independence of America's private, voluntary charities, and have long sought to bring them under greater control. The cause of the trouble is that the most important of the independent charities originate in religious faith, and the convictions of those faiths often directly conflict with the secular values of government. There was a spectacular recent example of this in San Francisco: the city government threatened to cut off its multimillion dollar contracts to the Catholic charities of the city unless the Roman Catholic church extended spousal benefits to the unmarried companions of its lay employees – including its homosexual employees. The result was even more spectacular: the Catholic church surrendered.

Those private charities that succeed most in pulling people from alcoholism, drug abuse, vagrancy or prostitution into some sort of orderly life – notably the Salvation Army – succeed, in my opinion, because they teach people the basic rules of a responsible life. These are: your life is what you make it, others will help you only if you live up to certain basic standards; charity is temporary; others help you out of kindness not because you have some right to their help; and you should turn for comfort in tough times not to narcotics but religious consolation. Needless to say, all of these lessons directly contradict the animating philosophy of the modern state.

But part of what President Clinton has in mind for the welfare reform era is closer integration of the state and voluntary charities – integration being a euphemism for supervision, direction, and ultimately control.

Monitoring the workings of welfare reform in practice and defending private charities against the state are, however, essentially defensive tasks. Political parties of the Right must find something more than this to do.

The passage of the welfare reform bill in the United States and the imminence of such a bill in Britain, even if phoney, does for a while remove from public concern the single most obnoxious feature of modern welfare state liberalism, while leaving in place many of the others. Disability programmes, like Supplementary Security Income (ssi) in the United States, are linked every bit as directly to the attack on work and Republican self-reliance as welfare. They are also linked to crime, because many of the mental disorders that express themselves in violence qualify one for ssi in the United

States. Some years ago I wrote a story for the *Wall Street Journal* about the men who spent the night in Pennsylvania Station. They were men who circulated in and out of prison, habitual users of alcohol or drugs, often running away from an arrest warrant in some other state. I talked to several dozen of them over the time I spent there, and found that the single most important source of income for them was SSI. In Britain, Europe and Canada, unemployment insurance has many of the same destructive consequences as welfare.

The future politics of welfare reform – for those who aspire to live in a society characterised by individualism, personal independence, respect for the rights of others and full and equal citizenship – is to help our fellow citizens see that welfare is not a bizarre exception to the general utility and morality of government aid. We need to convince our fellow citizens that the evil epitomised by welfare is the same evil that emerges from any government programme that delivers cash benefits to individuals above and beyond their direct personal contribution to those programmes: unemployment benefits that exceed the premiums paid in by that particular worker, old-age pensions that exceed the real value of the contributions to the national pension plan, indiscriminate programmes of disability aid and so on. This sounds like an enormous job. It is an enormous job. We may never see it finished. But who ever imagined that we would reach as far as we have already?

Chapter 5:
Charles Murray

Although it is always dubious how much influence any one book has, I know shortly after *Losing Ground* was published a reporter for the *Wall Street Journal* wanted to have a story for which the hook would be the way that it had become the Bible for the Reagan administration, and I was asked to name a list of people who had been deeply influenced by it. I told her that, as far as I knew, only one person, who happened to be a personal friend, in the entire administration had read the book. She went out, because her editor still wanted to do the story and reported back a couple of weeks later that I was right – no one in the Reagan administration had read *Losing Ground* and, in fact, they rather thought that it was all too radical a kind of proposition anyway. It worked its influence, if indeed it had any influence, much more indirectly.

This leads me to the issue I would like to discuss here: challenging the welfare consensus – something which I have made a living at now for about fifteen years. As the consensus has moved I have found that a way to continue making one's living is to move one's opinion and continue to challenge it. I would like to think this is not simply because I am a contrarian, but because I am discovering new truths.

In this chapter I will briefly go through what I see as the major shifts that have occurred in the welfare debate consensus so far, and include any observations on the British situation I have noticed since I have had the opportunity to come over here periodically since 1989 and take a look at it. I will look mostly at the future, because I think we are on the verge of a new kind of debate about the welfare system writ large that will be different in kind, or at least should be different in kind, from any debate we have thus far seen.

In general the thesis of my remarks is that the welfare debate has been moving gradually from what was originally a highly technocratic policy kind of debate about what does and does not work and what its effects are, to an increasingly philosophical debate about what we are trying to accomplish.

The debate began in the United States in the 1930s with the establishment of Aid to Families with Dependent Children (AFDC), the first American national welfare programme. The consensus which formed out of that debate persisted subsequently for about thirty years. I am aware that in Britain the welfare consensus goes back to Elizabethan times and the poor laws. The Americans were somewhat behind in this regard. But during those first thirty years there was generally, among people in the policy establishment and among intellectuals in general, a consensus that welfare was a modest effort to help people who were at the bottom of the heap through no fault of their own. That is how the AFDC was passed. People were helping women whose husbands had been killed in a mine accident, and sometimes women whose husbands had walked out on them.

The creator, Frances Perkins, one of the progenitors of the earliest legislation and subsequently Secretary of Labor in the Roosevelt administration, was absolutely appalled when she first heard that dependent women were going to be defined to include unmarried women, because it had not been part of any conception she had had regarding the purpose of the legislation.

That consensus, however, that help was given to those

who were at the bottom of the heap through no fault of their own, was only challenged by the most barren kind of curmudgeonly objection that it cost too much money and there were too many cheats.

The welfare queen was the emblem of the opposition in those first few decades. This refers to the woman who manages to convince the welfare department that she is six different women and so collects six different cheques, driving up in her Cadillac to collect them. It was people who were cheating, who were taking advantage of the system, that were seen as the problem. Welfare reform, if it was justified at all, was justified merely as a way of getting rid of the cheats.

In the early 1980s there was the beginning of a different kind of debate. It was this changing debate that *Losing Ground* was a part of. The consensus started to shift, based on the proposition that the problem with welfare was not how much it costs but what it has bought. The new argument said that there were consequences to the welfare system, not only in terms of women who were cheating, but also because of women who were playing by the rules which were devastating for society at large. This view lent itself to a great deal of caricature, so books like *Losing Ground* were portrayed as having women with pocket calculators figuring out the precise future discounted value of their welfare cheque and deciding whether or not to have a baby.

That was never the argument. Not in *Losing Ground* certainly. The argument was always much more powerful. It said that what the welfare system did, along with a variety of judicial decisions and changes in administrative procedures, was in effect to mask the long-term consequences of behaviour by cushioning the short-term costs. In doing so we had created not only a fundamentally changed environment in which young people made up their minds about what to do, but also a fundamentally changed environment in which they were raised.

So it is not necessary to support the argument that welfare contributes, let us say, to the illegitimacy ratio, nor to assume that in deciding whether to have sex in the back seat of the car people are always using the front part of their brain. All that it is necessary to assume is that if there is one kind of system where young women are brought up from early childhood with people constantly preaching to them, 'Do not dare get pregnant because the world is going to fall in on you if you do'; it is that kind of upbringing that has profound effects on the way people behave. Also, if young men are brought up believing that if they get a girl pregnant they have to marry her, then this also has a profound influence on how they behave. As a veteran of the 1950s I can attest to that personally.

The fact is that human beings, when they make decisions about such things as having sex, whether to look for a job, or how hard to look for a job, are acting out of a kind of reality check. That reality check often does not project very far into the future. It says, 'What is going to happen to me immediately if I engage in certain kinds of behaviour?' If there is one kind of answer, you get much more of a certain kind of behaviour than if there is another kind. The argument gained a lot of force during the 1980s, until, by the late 1980s, there was a new consensus that I can best summarise by saying that welfare dependency was a bad thing and people ought to be off welfare if they can. It does not sound like a revolution, but in fact it was.

In the 1970s people on the Left very seldom said that welfare dependency was in and of itself a bad thing. There was a much more *laissez-faire* attitude about making judgements about being on welfare at all. The Left, or at least the moderate Left, was prepared in the United States by the late 1980s to say that programmes which moved women from welfare to work were a good thing, that some forms of Workfare were beneficial. Meanwhile the conservatives, who were still often primarily concerned about how much welfare cost, also eagerly embraced this view of what was wrong with the system.

At the same time as this was going on, however, there was a shift in the position of those people who were opposed to welfare, and here I think I am a good example. As time went on in the 1980s I began to think less and less that the question was how to fix welfare. What came to the front of my mind, and to a variety of other analysts, was that the real problem that drives the underclass is illegitimacy – non-marital births, in the more politically correct formulation.

Communities in which large proportions of the children are born without fathers end up with enormous social problems. The 'kicker' to this point of view was that this is true whether or not the mothers are working. If a welfare reform bill succeeds in moving large numbers of women off the welfare rolls, but does nothing about the illegitimacy ratio, it has achieved nothing. There will be communities which experience the same kinds of problems that they now face with women who are single mothers but on welfare.

I first tried to make this case in Britain in 1989, when I met with what I think can gently be described as disbelief. In Britain there was an almost universal view that whether a woman has a baby out of wedlock or not is pretty much irrelevant. If that woman gets a decent level of support, it was thought that she could raise that child just as well as if she were in a traditional married relationship. After all, men are such brutes that sometimes it is better not to be married anyway. It has been fascinating for me to watch over the last seven years what I think is a perceptible shift in that position in Britain. I do not, by the way, attribute it to anything I have written. I think it is a consequence of watching the way the world works.

Watching council estates where there are large numbers of women who do not have husbands, seeing what life in those estates is like, and discovering the kinds of changes in society which have led an increasing number of people to believe that men do have a use in the raising of children, I have seen a shift in British attitudes. I believe it has gone much further in the United States.

When I first made the case in the United States that out-of-wedlock births were a bad thing, I had to really hunt hard for any empirical analyses on this issue in the technical literature. They were just not there. It was a question that had not been asked. So when I called up the person who managed a very large database in the United States and said that I was having trouble finding information as to whether births are out-of-wedlock or not, he replied that they did not record that factor because they saw it as irrelevant. That has changed now.

Recently I was in the position of doing what I periodically do, which is to go through a set of technical journals looking at all the titles and xeroxing all the articles that look to be of interest to me. I discovered in the course of the afternoon that I was starting to skip over articles detailing various kinds of bad consequences for children raised in single parent households; there was so much information it was getting redundant. In the United States the battle has been won intellectually.

This is exemplified by a leading liberal academic in the United States, Sarah McLanahan. At a conference I attended recently she said she was going to talk about the bad consequences of single parenthood for children, independently of money and income. She thought that the Left had a special responsibility to emphasise this, since, for so many years, they had denied these consequences existed. My jaw dropped. I did not know how to follow her. It was a very forthright and courageous statement on her part, but it reflects how far the intellectual debate has moved on.

The political consensus, however, has not moved nearly so far. It has stayed with an important dissenting element, largely focused on the issue of how can we get women off welfare. The 1996 Bill was crafted mostly in terms of ways of getting women off welfare. With the Left wanting to have more extensive job training and the Right being more willing to just have strict time limits, the measure of success continues to be what happens to AFDC rolls.

I am convinced that is the wrong measure of success. I believe that if there are going to be permanent long-term positive results from the current Welfare Reform Bill that was passed last year, it is going to be because a few states take advantage of the latitude the Bill gives them to make very substantial changes in who is eligible for assistance. It has always been my hope that some state somewhere – Utah might be the best candidate, or South Dakota or Montana where they have a small case load and also where the case load is mostly white – to avoid the whole issue of race – would simply cut off aid altogether to women under the age of eighteen. My expectation is that you would see large changes in behaviour, sharp reductions in the numbers of young women having babies under those circumstances without husbands, and that you would begin to have a creeping effect which would spread across the country. The absence of that kind of dramatic reform, in a few states, leaves me with a very gloomy prognosis for what is going to happen in the future.

It goes like this. Much of what enabled the reform of 1996 in the United States, and much of the reason why I think that welfare reform is still not at the very top of the public's agenda in Britain, even though the new administration considers it important, has to do with prosperity and falling unemployment rates. In the United States we can look at declining welfare loads and feel sanguine about the future because things seem to be working pretty well, and ignore the fact that many of those women who are getting those jobs right now are getting them because the job market is so tight.

If we assume that the business cycle has not been repealed, a safe assumption in my opinion, then we are looking at a recession some time in the next few years when the huge numbers of women who have got jobs are going to be back on the rolls again because they are by and large among the least productive workers. They are at the margins of the economy. At the same time there will be rising budget deficits because, lo and behold, the budget agreements that Congress is now making are loaded toward the back end, which means that all the reductions are not supposed to occur until a few years down the road. Also, the fact that it is going to be a balanced budget is based on projections that are not merely rosy but deep burgundy – projections that cannot possibly be true. So, there will be a rising deficit and rising joblessness, and an evaporation of the supposed gains of women getting off welfare. There is, however, going to be no increased enthusiasm for going back to the old consensus and saying, 'Oh well, just expand the welfare benefits because we are wrong after all'. The prospect, as far as I am concerned, is rather gloomy at this point.

I believe that the welfare reform consensus that led to the 1996 Bill has still not come to grips with the fact that changing the welfare system so that it accomplishes good is going to have to be done in ways which hurt people. Professor Digby Anderson from Britain wrote a book called *This Will Hurt*. It was a very well titled book about reform. If you are going to change the world so that people change their behaviour you cannot do it simply through carrots. You have to do it predominantly, I believe, on the issues that worry welfare reformers, i.e. through sticks.

Let us return to the case of out-of-wedlock births. It is not necessary to explain why young men want to sleep with young women, or why young women find babies attractive. These are phenomena that have very powerful driving forces behind them. What needs to be explained is why societies have been so effective in the past at constructing systems whereby the vast majority of children come into the world with two adults committed to their care. The answer, as far as I am concerned, is that you have some social rewards for behaving in that way, but an awful lot of penalties if you do not. If you slip off the straight and narrow path disaster awaits. You cannot reconstruct this kind of world without reconstructing to some extent a situation in which disaster awaits. There has been a real reluctance to come to grips with that. The only way you can come to grips with it, in my view, is if you think very hard and clearly about what you truly believe to be the morality of the situation.

Earlier I said that the debate has in the past been, I think, very technocratic – I think that it is still too technocratic. Let me propose the basic premises that I bring to it. You can then match that against your own view and get a sense of the kind of thinking that has to go on before we decide what we really ought to do about welfare.

My first proposition is that to bring a child into the world is just about the most important thing an ordinary human being can do. It is the action that is most laden with profound implications. My second premise is that to bring a child into the world that you are intellectually, emotionally or financially unable to care for is wrong. Unless people are prepared to say that this behaviour is wrong, I believe that it will be very difficult to come to grips with the appropriate public policy response. As long as people are constrained to think, 'We want to change the world, but we do not want to hurt anybody', and particularly, 'We do not want to hurt children', as long as people refuse to accept the fact that there are already millions of people being hurt very badly by the current system, no one will be able to think straight about what needs to be done.

As I said earlier, we are going to need a profound qualitative shift in the debate on the future of welfare. This is the longer term perspective. In the short term we have to face the problems of the oncoming recession, and how it will affect the debate. In the long term we should assume that the phenomenal increase in national wealth that has characterised both the United States and Britain is going to continue.

It is important to understand the degree of increase in that wealth. In the United States in 1900 – a time when the country was seen as Nirvana, when immigrants flocked to it because it was the richest country with the highest standard of living, along with Britain, of any country in the world – the median American household income for non-farm families was less than the current poverty line in real terms. As recently as 1940, on the verge of the Second World War, in excess of 40 per cent of American households fell below what we currently consider as the poverty line.

The implication of this is that, sometime not too far down the road, money will cease to be the same kind of constraining factor it has been in the past. Until now the welfare debate has been underwritten in large part by worries about money. Does it cost too much? Can we afford this?

Let me stipulate a future which could certainly exist. We have enough money that we could afford to take all the current social welfare programmes – in kind transfers and cash transfers – from one person to another, convert them to cash and give every American above the age of eighteen an income equal to half the median. This is not just putting them above the poverty line – half the median income has long been considered by social democrats as an ideal for income equality.

Let us suppose that there is enough money to put that much cash into everybody's pocket. Let us also imagine that we have determined what the negative work incentives would be of a guaranteed minimum income, and have ascertained that, even given those negative incentives, we can still sustain this system at levels of taxation that are no higher than, or perhaps are even lower than, the amount of money we are paying now with the panoply of programmes that we have. We now have, in effect, a no-cost option – no increased cost option, to eradicate poverty (financial poverty) absolutely once and for all.

But if we have the capacity to do that, is the majority in favour of doing it? It poses fascinating questions for both the Left and the Right. The Left has to be forced to come to grips in this case with something I believe most members of the Left understand, which is: if tomorrow everybody in the country is given an income that is more than enough to enable them to live a decent existence, large numbers of them will use that income in ways which prevent them from living a decent existence. People will gamble it away. They will use it on drugs. They will do this, that and the other thing. There will still be, the month after the guaranteed minimum income is in effect, large numbers of people living in squalor.

What does this mean for those on the Left? Does it mean that they do not want the guaranteed minimum income? Or, if they do have it, do they want to continue to supplement it with the welfare industry? Do they want to continue to have the welfare industry monitor the lives of the poor and try to bring them up from their counterproductive ways? If they do, what precisely are they saying about their attitude toward the autonomy of individual human beings? What precisely are they saying about egalitarianism? To what extent are they going to have to modify their own rhetoric about what they think of the capacities of the common man?

On the Right is an equally interesting set of challenges. I have stipulated that, in an economic sense, if there is a system which eradicates poverty, we can afford it. But it is also true that there are disincentives, so that, if you take the population as it exists after you have eradicated poverty through a guaranteed minimum income, you will have two sets of people. One set will be those who are better-off, these are people who, under any system – including a complete *laissez-faire* system in which there is no safety-net whatsoever – would continue to be unable to cope. If you got rid of the welfare system altogether, they would be the people who would be lying in the streets. Under a guaranteed minimum income they still are not going to lead a very good life, but let us say that at least they are going to have a cheque coming every month so that they can keep going in a way that is better than it was before.

You are also going to have another group of people who, in a society where there was no safety-net whatsoever, would live lives of dignity and autonomy. They would get into the job market and would stay there. They would earn decent incomes. They would raise families and children and, in the process of doing all that, they would lead lives which give them the kinds of deep, rich sources of satisfaction that are, in effect, the same sources of satisfaction that most of us use as the measure of our lives. That is in the absence of any safety-net. Given a guaranteed minimum income, or given a lavish welfare state of any kind, some set of that population will not live that kind of life. They will either not get jobs at all, or they will get in and out of the labour market and condemn themselves to perpetual menial jobs. They will not marry, or they would have married before. If they have children they will not be children that they take care of. They will be forty, fifty, sixty years old and miserable in the kinds of ways that have nothing to do with money. This is a second population of people.

It is important for conservatives then to think about how their view of a welfare state is affected by what the relative size of those two populations is likely to be. I recently wrote a book called *What it Means to be a Libertarian*, in which, in the first draft, I had a chapter on the welfare state where I proposed the guaranteed minimum income. It contained a *quid pro quo*. We will give the Left an end to poverty and in return let us eradicate the apparatus of the welfare state.

Milton Freedman proposed this a long time ago as not a perfect, but the best available solution to the problem of providing for people in need. In my chapter, I wrote, 'Yes, I do not think it is perfect, but I am willing to go along with it'. After doing it, I looked at it. I thought about the size of those two populations of people I have just described and I said, 'No'. In my own heart of hearts, the way I believe society would work would be: first, that the population of people from whom we would be stripping a meaningful life is going to be very large, and second, that the population of people who would be marginally better-off would be absent and any welfare state whatsoever is going to be extremely small.

I have a great deal of confidence in a rich nation being able to deal through civil society with the human needs that would remain if you had no safety-net at all. Because of my estimation of the size of those populations, and my estimations of what it means to live a satisfying human life, I wrote a next version of the chapter in which I advocated getting rid of everything: social security, AFDC, subsidies to agriculture, the whole lot. But I had to go through that process in order to reach this conclusion.

In a much larger context this is what is going to face both Britain and the United States, if not in the next ten years then in twenty, thirty or forty years' time. We are going to be able to afford almost any kind of system we want, and we will finally have to decide what kind of system it is that we want which in turn must be posited on an excruciating re-examination of what is the dependent variable in which we are interested.

What is the measure of success that we apply to social policy? When I see it as something for the future, my subtext should be obvious. I believe that also is the topic that should ultimately dominate our thinking today.

The idea that the welfare system is a matter of money has largely, if not completely, died. It has been supplemented by a very strong understanding that we are engaged in a never-ending process of trying to say what it is that governments can and cannot do for human beings. I am pleased to see that people are discussing today the kind of progress that can be made. Whether this will continue is another question. There are many incentives for all of us to duck these issues. I will continue to hope, but I do remember Samuel Johnson's injunctions about 'triumphs of hope over experience'.

Chapter 6:
Anthony Coles

For too long New York City was a model of how not to get things done. So it is particularly gratifying that it is now held up as an example of a city that is working. New York has changed. Times have changed. We have reinvented our government and the way we deliver governmental services. We have become a city where new ideas are welcomed and actually put to the test. We are always thinking and we are always looking for solutions. The Manhattan Institute has been a very important part of the city's success. They have served as an intellectual bridge for many of the policies we are trying to put into practice. We are all very grateful for that.

One result of this reclaiming of New York's rightful place is the frequent statements by our Mayor that New York City is the 'capital of the world': 'Albany may be the capital of New York State. Washington DC may be the capital of the United States. But New York City is the capital of the world.'

Needless to say, we receive letters from people all around the world, claiming that this is not the case. One of my responsibilities was to reply to these letters, which was somewhat hard to do. After a while I just gave up. However, in 1995 the Pope came to visit New York City. He gave a mass in Central Park and before the mass he said, 'Mayor Giuliani, it is a pleasure to be here in the capital of the world.' Now my response is easy: 'Don't take it up with me. Don't take it up with the Mayor. Take it up with the Pope.'

So, what was New York City like in January 1994 when we first took office. There were 1.2 million individuals on welfare which is one in six people in New York City. It was detrimental for the recipients who were not forced to work, who were receiving a welfare cheque and doing nothing in return. And it was detrimental for the city. In fact, it was a sign of the city moving in the wrong direction.

What was particularly puzzling for us was that there was no thought on how to address the problem. Over the four years leading up to 1994 New York City had probably seen a steeper increase in the welfare rolls than at any other time in the city's history. Government had no answers. It was just looking for more money in order to fund the increase, from additional taxes, the state government or the federal government. The future path for welfare in the city was set. If you were to follow its course, in five or six years everybody in the city would have been on welfare. So the Mayor set about finding a solution – one which did not simply involve asking for more money. He addressed it in a larger context of city management.

What was happening in New York, and in other urban areas, was that substandard behaviour was becoming standard behaviour, in Senator Moynihan's famous phrase, the city was 'defining deviancy down', it was essentially choking off hope in New York City. People did not want to live there any more and were questioning whether or not cities still had a role to play in their future lives.

The Mayor was convinced that restoring a sense of civic pride would not only reclaim and re-establish the city but also affirm the basic tenets of the social contract. He set about generating in our welfare programme, and also in the city, a sense of reciprocal responsibility. For every benefit there was an obligation. For every right there was a responsibility. Simple concepts, but concepts that New York had lost.

The key component in re-establishing the social contract was the Workfare programme. It puts people to work, promotes personal responsibility, creates confidence and says to the citizen that he must give something back in return for the benefit he is receiving from others. It also puts into practice the theory that the best training for a job is a job.

Before I describe exactly how the programme was implemented, I will briefly outline the structure of welfare in New York City. There are two programmes. One is the federal programme, Aid to Families with Dependent Children, AFDC. Essentially this is a welfare benefit for families with children. As part of New York State the city also has a second programme, a general assistance system, called 'Home Relief'. On the whole, it is for single, able-bodied individuals. Both cost the city and the state money, although in different degrees.

In March 1995, there were 863,000 individuals on the AFDC programme. On Home Relief there were about 277,000. The average grant for a family of three on the AFDC programme is $1,613. For Home Relief it was $886, including other benefits, such as food stamps and some medical programmes as well. The new system we instituted had three essential parts to it. There was a strict verification of the people who were applying for welfare; a Workfare programme, and an effort to place people in work after they completed the programme.

The essence of the first part, the evaluation, was called 'EVR', Evaluation Verification and Review. The core of it consisted of interviews with everybody who applied for assistance. We tried to make sure that each applicant genuinely deserved the assistance in order to reduce the number of fraudulent claims. We made home visits and financial checks. If people did not pass the EVR process, they did not get on the rolls.

In addition, we implemented a system of 'finger imaging', a computer form of fingerprinting. The aim was to reduce duplication in the rolls. We found that some people were claiming welfare two, three, or four times. People from other states were receiving welfare grants from elsewhere as well as from New York, and we wanted to reduce this. There were rigorous interviews, home visits, finger imaging and then, before anyone could go on the rolls, they had to attend one of our employment centres. The employment centres organise mandatory employment activity which aims to divert people from the rolls. It is a thirty-day programme where, under supervision, potential recipients are asked to telephone potential interviewers, send out CVs and do all that they can in order to get a job.

Finally, we also set up a process called, 'Intensive Case Control'. Under Intensive Case Control each supervisor was assigned a welfare worker, who made sure that each welfare recipient completed all the necessary steps in order to qualify for the benefit. If the potential recipient failed to follow each of the steps they would not get on the welfare rolls.

As a result of this programme we reduced the acceptance rate for welfare in New York from 80 per cent to 50 per cent in two years.

The reasons people were disqualified are interesting. They

also support the belief that the programme is now being administered more rationally. The main reasons why people did not qualify were, first, because they had other income (about 23 per cent); second, because they gave a false address (20 per cent); and, third, because they withdrew from the programme (around 18 per cent). We assumed they withdrew because they could not meet the other standards that we were holding out for the programme. This means that in total almost 60 per cent of applicants either withdrew, had other income or gave a false address.

The second part of the programme is the Workfare element. This is a key part. Recipients are required to work for their benefits. In Home Relief the initial requirement is twenty-six hours a week. If you are on AFDC it is twenty hours a week. If you are on AFDC and we require you to work, we also supply childcare. So no one is required to work if they have a child, unless childcare is also provided.

Today there are approximately 40,000 welfare recipients working for New York City and for various non-profit making organisations. This, of course, is a significant undertaking by the city but one that, in our view, is well worth it. It creates a sense of discipline and social order in the city and again, we believe, giving people work is the best training that there is for a job. If somebody is in a job and they want training we would encourage that. However, training programmes, we believe, should be available to supplement work experience and not to substitute for it.

Finally, the third element of the programme is an effort to get people who are participating in our Workfare programme actual jobs. We do this through a division we have organised called 'Business Link'. Business Link operates as an employment centre for our Workfare population. Today it has approximately 100 participating companies from the private sector who have either hired Workfare workers, or have considered hiring Workfare workers. In the sixteen months it has been in operation around 1,500 people have been hired for work. This is not that high a number when you look at the size of our case load but it is certainly a step in the right direction.

As a result of our programme how has the city improved? First and foremost, since March 1995, when we first put the programme into effect, we have reduced the welfare rolls by 22 per cent. The rolls have decreased from about 1.1 million to about 900,000. This is a significant reduction – to put it in context, it is about half the population of Sheffield and more than half the population of Liverpool. It is probably more than the welfare population in most other states in the United States. New York is now a cleaner city, one that is beginning to internalise a sense of civic pride, a sense of the social contract and a sense that for every right there is a corresponding duty.

There is also less crime and less homelessness. Many of the programme's critics said that if people were taken off welfare the result would be an increase in crime and homelessness. That has not been the case. We have found, by concentrating on the welfare programme, managing the city as a whole and restoring the sense of the social contract, we have reduced welfare, reduced homelessness and reduced crime. New Yorkers believe that the city, for all these reasons, is now moving in the right direction.

Chapter 7:
James Miller

Very few people have been to Wisconsin unless it is by chance. Now, however, it is playing a large role in politics which I will describe in this chapter.

In January 1987, when Tommy Thompson was sworn in as governor of Wisconsin, there were 3,735,386 families receiving AFDC in the United States. By September 1996 the case load had increased to 4,267,926 throughout the country – a rise of 14 per cent. During that time twenty-nine states saw their case loads rise. The two largest states, California and Texas, saw increases of 49 per cent and 55 per cent respectively. Some of the smaller states, such as New Hampshire, Arizona and Nevada, saw the case loads increase by more than 100 per cent.

On the other hand, twenty-one states saw the number of case loads drop. Most of these decreases were small. The state with the second largest decrease was Michigan, which had a fall of 22 per cent.

I am going to discuss the state with the largest decreasing case load, Wisconsin. We went from 98,295 cases in January 1987 to 49,930 cases in September 1996. A staggering fall of 49 per cent. I will examine some of the reasons why welfare reform has worked in Wisconsin and how Wisconsin is driving the welfare debate in the United States. To understand why Wisconsin has been able to achieve these extraordinary welfare case reductions, we must take a look at the state's unique history and place in American social policy.

In the 1870s a scholar named John Bascombe was president of the University of Wisconsin. Towards the end of his life Bascombe wrote a book called *Sociology*. In it he laid out the view of how the world would change, and the moral imperative of government to become the most important source of services and direction for the common citizen. In reality, this book and Bascombe's theories as a whole became the early foundation of what would later become known as the 'Nanny State'.

One of Bascombe's protégés was a young student named Robert Le Folla who, in the early twentieth century, would become leader of the progressive movement in the United States and would run for President in 1924 on a platform of major reform. These two men started Wisconsin on a path towards developing social policies that would have a direct effect upon the entire country.

Many of the ideas in social policy came directly from Madison, Wisconsin's state capital. It is one of the great ironies in American public policy that for a century the idea of big government came from a small state in the heartland, but in the last decade of the twentieth century a new conservative view would rise from the very same place and begin to dismantle the liberal ideology of big government.

But it has not just been in the area of welfare reform that the impact of the new Wisconsin ideas have been felt. There are issues such as educational choice, ending parole in the criminal justice system, and putting spending caps on local property taxes. Wisconsin has moved rapidly during the last decade to make major social policy changes that have been emulated by other states across America. I will, however, focus on the issue of welfare. In no area has Wisconsin had a greater impact during the last ten years than in the government's role in the lives of poor people.

The many voices in the welfare debate reached a crescendo in Wisconsin in the mid-1980s. This was not so much because of the rising spiral in costs of welfare benefits, but because of an issue that was in some respects unique to Wisconsin: interstate welfare migration.

In the early 1980s migration to Wisconsin by welfare recipients from such cities such as Gary, Indiana and Chicago began. Mothers discovered that the actual economic benefits of welfare were much higher in Wisconsin than they were in their home states of Indiana and Illinois. This was also noticed by welfare recipients in the southern states, such as Mississippi and Arkansas. As the number on the welfare rolls began to rise, specifically in Milwaukee, this migration caused greater public anger towards welfare – more so in Wisconsin than in any other state.

In 1985 the governor of Wisconsin was a Liberal Democrat called Tony Earl. In a situation not at all dissimilar to 1992, in the presidential race, Republicans thought Earl to be unbeatable for a second term in 1986. The leading Republican candidates, whom I would describe as 'The A-Team', decided not to run. So it was left to several little-known Republicans to enter a primary for the reward of being trounced in the 1986 election.

One of these was a small town legislator named Tommy Thompson. He had been a minority leader in the Wisconsin legislature, but he was not thought to be a heavy hitter, or someone who would ever seriously be considered for governor. However, in 1986 circumstances began to change rapidly and the issue causing the change was welfare.

In early 1986 Republicans began making serious charges

concerning the entire welfare structure in the state of Wisconsin. One of their key charges was that welfare immigration from other states was driving up the cost for Wisconsin taxpayers. Wisconsin operates on a biannual budget. By January 1986 there was a looming deficit of $340 million. By constitutional mandate Wisconsin is not allowed budget deficits, so the issue became a real problem for the incumbent.

Governor Earl, who had been committed to increasing spending for welfare, suddenly found himself with few political allies and began to back-pedal on possible welfare increases. He froze welfare payments. In April 1986 he signed legislation creating a Workfare pilot programme for five Wisconsin counties. Meanwhile the Republicans continued to pound away at the entire issue of welfare. Thompson became the Republican nominee and proposed a 5 per cent cut in AFDC benefits, to be followed by a benefit freeze until neighbouring states caught up with Wisconsin's generous level of welfare payments. He also stressed the need to increase work requirements for recipients.

What is important to understand concerning the politics surrounding this issue is that the Wisconsin counties experiencing the greatest AFDC rises were in fact the heart of the Democratic vote in Wisconsin. Welfare, as an issue, became a disaster for Democratic candidates because it was their voters who were most upset with the existing welfare policies.

One month before the election, Governor Earl accused Tommy Thompson of wanting to be governor of Mississippi i.e. wanting to provide second-rate government services.

Thompson, in a classic reply, said, 'I won't have to run for governor of Mississippi. With our generous welfare payments all the people from Mississippi are moving up here.' Late in the campaign, as public opinion began to shift away from the liberal incumbent, Governor Earl pledged to freeze benefits for two years in the next budget, and set a goal of cutting welfare case loads by 20 per cent in 1991. It was too late. On November 4th 1986 a small-town Republican, who had been given little chance of becoming governor of Wisconsin, won over the liberal incumbent by 54 per cent to 46 per cent. Welfare policy in the United States would never be the same.

My Institute was founded in 1987, during Governor Thompson's first year in office. One of our first projects was to begin a state-wide public opinion survey. Starting with the first survey, and continuing over the next decade, we have interviewed more than 15,000 Wisconsin residents. Our first survey was conducted by the Gordness Black Corporation which owns Lewis Harris and is an internationally known public opinion firm.

In the survey Wisconsin residents ranked the problem of welfare second only to taxes as the most important issue in the state. An astounding 28 per cent regarded it as a serious problem on an open-ended question. In those times in the United States it was unheard of to get even 10 per cent on a state poll naming welfare as a serious problem.

This survey questioned 1,000 randomly selected Wisconsin residents. Our findings on welfare – note, this was 1987 – were the following:

- 83 per cent of the respondents felt the size of welfare encouraged migration to the state
- 84 per cent believed that the existing welfare system actually increased poverty
- 87 per cent believed that the welfare rolls contained many people who could work, but did not
- 91 per cent believed that persons who receive welfare should be required to take available employment
- 94 per cent felt that welfare recipients should be required to take jobs, job training or attend school.

Those familiar with public opinion surveys will recognise that these types of numbers are amazing, especially when you consider that in the mid-1980s it was still considered politically incorrect to talk about welfare reform.

I must report, however, that there was one other percentage in that 1987 survey that has not changed over the last ten years. It is something to remember when you talk about the future of welfare reform. That figure is 96 per cent. It represents the overwhelming majority of Wisconsin residents who believe in the concept of providing welfare benefits to people who are in need and who cannot support themselves. Then and now people in Wisconsin believe there is an obligation to help the poor, but with a welfare system that works.

Beginning in 1987 Governor Thompson began a series of specific reforms aimed at changing the welfare system forever. That year welfare benefits were reduced by 6 per cent and frozen at the new level. Also, a programme called Learnfare was proposed and implemented. It mandated that

AFDC families could be penalised when children were truant from school. During the next several years, welfare policy began to change in Wisconsin. It remained a major issue in Wisconsin politics and it continued to cut into the large Democratic core counties in the eastern part of the state, especially in Milwaukee.

In 1990 Governor Thompson was re-elected by a landslide. By 1993 the Democrat-controlled legislature became so frustrated with the issue of welfare that it decided to pass Act 99, which called for termination of the state's participation in AFDC, and the establishment of a work self-sufficiency based reform programme. The legislature never believed that Governor Thompson would sign it. They believed this type of legislation would embarrass him and take some of the pressure off welfare reform, because Thompson had never indicated any plans for a long-term reform programme. Unfortunately for the Democrats, Thompson signed the bill.

By 1996 the new programme called 'Wisconsin Works' or 'W2' was enacted. In September 1997 AFDC, as we have known it for several generations, ceased to exist in Wisconsin. It has been replaced by a system that demands that recipients of government aid be required to work for their benefits.

I would like to stress one thing. The real welfare metamorphosis in Wisconsin is from total entitlement to personal responsibility. Today the immediate focus is on the issue of jobs. What happens to poor people? What happens to their children? These are all legitimate issues. But what Thompson did in Wisconsin, and what is happening across the United States at warp speed, is that the entire issue of entitlement has been put to rest in terms of welfare reform.

A decade ago, when one mentioned 'reform' and 'welfare', one would associate it with a barrage of charges, such as 'racism' and 'insensitivity'. That is no longer the case. Personal responsibility has now been introduced into the issue of welfare reform and been universally accepted. If a poor person is to receive a benefit cheque, he or she has an obligation to perform a productive service for society. This was never the intention of entitlements. This change in human behaviour is still the single most important feature in welfare reform.

And so, a decade later, what has 'welfare reform' meant to Wisconsin? Some changes are obvious. Before the welfare reform came, our case loads would have been expected to grow from approximately 100,000 in 1986 to approximately 135,000 by 1996. In reality Wisconsin's case load decreased to 50,000.

Rather than spending more money we have produced huge savings. When these figures are adjusted for inflation we have cut our spending by one-third in real dollars. We have established that the age of welfare entitlement is over. We have also, however, understood something that was in our first original survey: that Wisconsin citizens, like most Americans, still believe we have a moral obligation to help poor people. But it must be a system that encourages work, self-sufficiency and social responsibility.

There are, of course, those who will point out some of the obvious flaws in the Wisconsin story, one of which is the disparity in the case load reductions in Milwaukee County versus the remainder of the state. This happens to be true. While some counties have experienced a decrease in case loads of 70 per cent to 80 per cent during the last ten years, Milwaukee's figures trail at 25 per cent.

It is also true that many of our counties do not have large minority populations, while Milwaukee has a growing central city and would be similar to most cities across America. I would like to point out, however, that Milwaukee's decrease of 25 per cent ranks it above any other city in the ten-year period. It is true that we are about to confront a portion of the welfare population that some studies have labelled as dysfunctional. By most estimates it is placed at approximately 30 per cent of the current case loads.

It is also correct to say that, because of our earlier successes, we are likely in the future to have smaller decreases than other states. On Wednesday May 7th 1996 the *New York Times* had a major front page story on the welfare reforms taking place in Milwaukee. The clear purpose of its research was to paint an alarming picture of the lives of the poor in Milwaukee. After extensive interviews, unhappily, they were forced to conclude:

> The mere absence of obvious calamities is seen in some
> quarters as a reason for cautious optimism. A first
> tentative suggestion is that as welfare restrictions sweep
> the cities, many poor people will find ways to adapt.

The descriptions of Milwaukee's recent welfare statistics are similar to the ones quoted throughout this paper. In another issue of the *New York Times* concerning Milwaukee, they wrote:

> Case loads have shrunk nearly 25 per cent in the last year
> alone. In each month another 1,800 people leave the
> system. No major city has ever seen such startling major
> declines, though many are now looking here with an
> envious eye in the hope of imitation.

There is, however, a clear understanding in my state, backed by legislation, that we will never return to the old system of simple handouts. Poor people are best served by being treated like adults. Our current system encourages adult behaviour by stressing social responsibility and the need to work for any benefits given by the state. We also understand that, with the introduction of w2, some of our social service spending will actually increase in the short term. This is an investment we feel is worth making, because we also firmly believe that we must provide the tools to help a generation of poor people relearn the cultural value of work and make a positive contribution to our society. We hope this is a new Wisconsin idea.

In Britain there is not a clear understanding of the roles of governors in American public policy. In 1994 there was a tremendous upheaval in the American political system. The Republicans were swept to victory. Congress took over both Houses. But at the same time there were huge elections of Republican governors across the country. Today, of America's fifteen largest states fourteen have governors who are Republicans. The fifteenth is Florida where the governor is retiring. More importantly, when these governors were elected in 1994 the margins of victory were huge. I do not mean by a few per cent. I mean that people were winning with margins of 30 to 40 per cent. It gave them the mandate to start making radical changes. It is true that Wisconsin has been in the lead, but there is a group of states that are implementing exceptional changes now. A lot of people do not recognise how fast some of these reforms are going through.

Another fact about governors in America is that, by constitutional statute at state level, they have to have balanced budgets. They cannot run deficits. They have to be very serious with reforms and the reforms, short term and long term, have to work financially.

What is happening in America is that more and more reforms occur at the local level, especially in the areas of social policy. I fully support this and would argue that welfare reform now is coming from the states to Washington, rather than the other way around.

I would also point out that in the last six American presidential elections, five of the winners were former governors. People in the United States have a sense of governors actually doing something and are very supportive of them. It looks like the Republican governors elected in 1994 will be successful again in 1998. In Wisconsin a liberal newspaper recently wrote a headline that Governor Thompson seems to be in trouble because the new polls showed him dropping 10 points in favourability and job performance. He now stands at 70 per cent.

Chapter 8:
Peter Cove

I am going to discuss the day-to-day reality of how to get someone from welfare to work.

My company, America Works, is a welfare-to-work business which now operates in four American cities: New York, Baltimore, Indianapolis and Albany, and I have put forward several proposals to bring America Works-type programmes to Britain. The welfare problems that exist in both countries do not substantially differ and neither, in my opinion, will the solutions.

As a company we recruit people who are on welfare. We give them a very small amount of training for between six to seven weeks. The training is not designed to change the effects of bad education on a person's capacity, but to give people the ability to begin to understand the workplace and what it is like. Fitting into the workplace is, I believe, the major issue of welfare to work.

Once they have had six or seven weeks of learning things such as how to fill out a CV, how to conduct oneself in an interview — look people in the eye, do not say things you should not, say things you should — we give them some familiarity with job areas. During these weeks they acquire familiarity in the industries where we have customers who will go on to hire welfare recipients from us.

We also have a sales force similar to Manpower or Kelly Services. They will bang on doors and ask if there are any jobs that are available. If there are, our sales force will find out if they will interview some of our people and, if they like them, whether they will take them almost as a temp for four months and pay us while we pay the worker. At the end of the four months, if the customer is happy and hires that person, and the person succeeds in the workplace, then the government will pay us for having done what we said we would, getting someone off welfare.

Our companies only take on people who are ready to work, because we are very careful to select those who want to work and screen out those who do not. We cannot do anything with people who do not want to work, but we can be successful with people who do. I have worked in this business for thirty years and believe that most people on welfare, when given the opportunity and the right kind of transition, want to work, can work and will be successful at working.

During the period of time they are in a job placement – while they are on trial if you like – we do something which I believe is central to the success of any welfare-to-work programme. We help with the transition from dependence and welfare to independence and work. We work with people to resolve the issues that could prevent them successfully working in that job.

There will be numerous factors that can get in the way of their success. Education and training tend not to be the major issue. What is more of a barrier is what I call 'static'. Many people on welfare have this static. It could be an abusive spouse at home, lack of transportation, a sick child, a day-care issue, not understanding the norms of the workplace, not understanding what to do when you have run out of things to do on the job – do you sit and read a book or ask for more work? What do you do when someone asks you to do something that you either find offensive, or is not part of your job description? How do you behave in the workplace?

In the main, the people coming off welfare, certainly in the United States, have been so disassociated from the means of production in our country that they no longer understand what it is like to be an employee and have no role models. They do not understand what it is like to work.

We send someone to the worksite every single week to work with our client's line manager in the company. If they have a willing worker who is experiencing problems integrating into the workplace, we provide the intervention that will assist them in moving from welfare to work. It is not mollycoddling. It is in no way giving them something they should not have. Rather, it is about giving them the ability to succeed when they want to. We are very rigorous in turning down those who do not want to succeed. We have performance reviews every single week so people know if they are performing or not. It is tough love but it works.

The state of New York tracks our people at America Works in New York City and Albany, New York. Fifteen months after we have placed them in a job, in New York City 80 per cent of the people are still off welfare. In Albany, New York, 92 per cent are still off welfare, having spent an average of five years on it before coming to America Works. The percentage is higher in Albany because of those who have been mandated to come to work – I will return to this later.

America Works is only paid if it succeeds. One of the problems that we have had – certainly in the United States, and I believe in Britain as well – is that welfare-to-work programmes have traditionally been financed regardless of their success. In fact in the United States there is a cardinal rule: if a programme does not work you double its funding, because clearly the reason it did not work was that it did not have enough money in the first place. We believe the problem should be approached in a very different way. America Works has forced municipalities to face issues such as what it is worth to get someone off welfare and how much it is worth to society to do this successfully.

In New York state, the governor has decided on a figure of $5,000. If welfare recipients do not get off benefit, we do not get paid. If they do get off, we do get paid but only when the government has made the money back. I have to get paid or else I go out of business. This is very unusual for welfare-to-work programmes. As I said before, usually when they fail they receive more money.

What I suggest as a policy implication of what America Works does in the States, and what we are hoping to see here in Britain, is that training providers – they could be non-profit-making – should be allowed to take on some of the responsibility of moving people from welfare to work on a guaranteed basis. If they do not succeed in finding the person a job they do not get paid. If they do find the person a job and they stay on in that job long enough to make the savings to the government, the provider should be paid.

In this environment you would begin to develop a market place of providers, paid by results, who deliver to the private sector workers who are ready and want to work. Some would operate like America Works – I think that some elements in our programme, particularly, the on-the-job counselling, should be part of any programme. But there would be room for other models involving unions, colleges or whoever. All you need to do is put incentives out there and pay those who are responsible for getting people to work and off welfare according to their results.

In America this is already beginning to happen on quite a significant scale. I would now like to see it happen in Britain. Then we could begin to sort out the kind of techniques which are most effective in moving people from welfare to work.

One question that I am frequently asked is why the private sector wants welfare recipients. Why do they hire them and why would they like to have them? The answer is that if you can get someone who is ready to work to the private sector, in many cases that is all they really need, or all they can expect, given the state of education and training and education programmes. About four years ago, I was asked by Daniel Patrick Moynihan to put together a group of private companies to discuss what public policies would increase the private sector's uptake in hiring welfare recipients. There were representatives from about a dozen firms – from small to international companies – sitting around a table. For about three hours we discussed the options and they said they didn't want tax incentives or wage subsidies or education and training programmes. They wanted people who were ready to work. The training could come later.

Recently I was at a conference with President Clinton. He came up to me and said that there should be an America Works in every city in America. He talked about the need for tax credits to encourage private companies to hire welfare recipients. We know in our country that tax credits to private companies just do not work in terms of getting people into work. So even the President, who has pushed for welfare reform, who would love to see America Works operating across the country, still does not fully understand. What works is making people ready to work. Only then will private companies hire them.

Chapter 9:
Frank Field

I want to outline the contours, as I see them, of the welfare debate unfolding in the country over the medium and longer term. There are, I think, three parts to the debate. The first is the framework of events and ideas. The second is the first principles from which I will be working and about which I am thinking. The final and main part is about strategies to counter dependency and low income.

First, the framework of ideas. One can polarise crudely the debate over welfare reform in this country and elsewhere between two views. The first says you can explain the increase in the numbers of people on benefit by what has been happening in the wider economy both nationally and globally. The second says the rise in dependency – noticeable in this country and in others, particularly America – is to do with human motivation, the sorts of people who are on welfare, and deep issues about their character. I think that both views offer partial explanations for the numbers of people on the welfare rolls in Britain today.

I would be presenting a very incomplete picture if I ignored what has been happening in the wider society over, let us say, the last fifteen or twenty years – not to trying to make a political point out of it. It is important to bear in mind that since 1979 one-third of all manufacturing jobs in this country has been wiped out. Overwhelmingly these were jobs which employed males. While some people might dispute the adequacy of the wages these jobs paid, they were the bedrock on which couples built their families and set about raising and nurturing children.

Of course if we look at the crude employment totals we see that there has been a large increase in the numbers of jobs after that first massive haemorrhage in manufacturing. But the composition of those jobs is different from those they replaced and it is the nature of many of these new jobs which helps to explain the inequalities in the distribution of work, which is now more marked than it was, say, twenty years ago.

Some people lay great stress on changes in the distribution of personal income. I put equal, if not greater, weight on the distribution of household income, and am concerned about the unequal access to new jobs when they are created. I am also concerned about the pay levels of those jobs and how they interact with the benefit system. It may go a long way to explaining why we have a growth of households where nobody works, and households where there may be two, three, four or more wage packets coming in. These economic changes are hugely significant in their impact on some families' well-being.

But there is also a second factor: the impact that the provision of welfare has on how people behave. I have always found it strange that so many people who get excited about the dangers of smoking and how important it is to stop people smoking, at the same time believe that you can spend £100 billion on welfare without influencing people's behaviour at all. I believe it *does* affect people's behaviour. How it affects it is the relevant question to ask. The task of the new Labour government is to understand rather than to condemn. The situation we find ourselves in is not generally man-made, but the product of actions by successive governments. I am not in the business of blaming the victims when we, as politicians, should be looking much more seriously at our part in bringing about a tax and benefit system which has done so much to work against the verities we·wish to see advanced.

The third aspect of the framework agenda is a belief about the reaction of taxpayers to all this. It links in to what I want to talk about in terms of strategies. To borrow those memorable words of Lord Penn about the imminent death of George V, the age of the quiet taxpayer is peacefully drawing towards its close. The time when we, as politicians, can happily put our hands into taxpayers' pockets and draw out what we want is passing.

I do not want anyone to have the impression that Labour think taxpayers will finance all that we wish to do. Indeed, our mandate extends from accepting and being elected on a very clear platform of financial restraint. It means that my department – and I am sure other departments too – are having to think much more carefully about how budgets are spent, what our objectives are, and how those objectives can be fulfilled using existing resources.

As far as the first principles within the framework are concerned, there seem to be four fundamental questions which we need to answer:

- what is the nature of welfare, what constitutes it and how should we define it?
- what underpins that provision?
- what values should welfare be teaching and what values should it not be teaching?
- how can welfare once again become an engine force for a social advance and betterment?

These questions ought to give more than just a clue about what I see as one of the most important roles of government: to understand those forces and institutions in our society which advance the condition of the people and their social well-being. We look to government to foster and nurture those institutions, rather than cripple and destroy them.

The last area I want to address is the strategies for advance. I say 'strategies' in the plural, not in the singular. There is no one magic wand, or witch-doctor's set of clothes in which we can dress ourselves, dance around and think something will happen. There are five strategies that I see. First, we want to rebuild mass support for welfare in the country. That is why the first principal question I posed earlier about the nature of welfare will be so important. It also highlights a change of emphasis for the Centre Left. If you look at the success of Clement Attlee in building support for the welfare state, it was based on the fact that the poor and the working class were, as often as not, interchangeable terms in those days. Nobody had any doubts that his policies were about underpinning the living standards of the vast majority of people in this country.

Over time the emphasis on the welfare state began to change. Its widespread appeal began to shrink, people no longer naturally associated themselves with the welfare state because they, like in a previous incarnation, began to see welfare as that which only or mainly concerned the poor. I want to remove welfare from that ghetto and to rebuild its broad-based support.

Second, we want to cut the supply routes into long-term

dependency and the descent into hopelessness for those who are already there. David Blunkett, the Education Secretary, has already set about this by trying to raise the standards and achievements of individual pupils, and combat failure in individual schools which can have such an impact on children. Among young people there are two very vulnerable groups. One is those young men who in times past would have expected to leave school with minimal skills but who would have found a reasonable job with reasonable rewards in the manufacturing sector, which is now much shrunk. If people graduate from school now without possessing the most basic numeracy and literacy, or IT and social skills, they risk slipping into long-term dependency.

The other vulnerable group are young girls who go on to be young mothers. We know from the National Child Development Study who these people are likely to be. They are those girls who feel they never achieved at school – whether it is at primary or secondary school – but also girls who are successes at junior school, but who fail to sustain that success in secondary school. Overwhelmingly, very young mothers come from these two groups. Raising performance and achievement in our schools, then, is not only about recognising the importance and sacredness of every individual, but also about more mundane reasons – stopping people being recruited into long-term dependency on welfare.

Our third strategy is for managing the reform programme itself. If we are to copy any system I hope it will be the Lloyd George model. The government must have confidence about the direction in which we believe we should head, but we must match that with the humility to learn about how our goals can best be achieved. We will be laying down our general principles and having as wide a debate as possible, both with our colleagues in parliament, with interested parties and, above all, with the country itself. In this way the reform programmes will be much more effective than they would be if we worked them out in private and then launched them on an unsuspecting public.

The fourth aim is easier to articulate than to achieve, but it is important to spell it out from the beginning so that we can be held to account on it. It is to move from a system which large numbers of people see as one of forced dependency, to a system based on opportunity. As one single mother explained to me, having read about our various proposals, she was so pleased we were going to move to a welfare state which gave a hand-up rather than a put-down. She felt that in the past she was always trying to take the initiative herself, but that she would be put down by the rules, the regulations, the officials and the law. Of course it will be difficult to make the transition from dependency to opportunity, but it is a very important objective.

The last strategy concerns the mechanisms of social advance. It is a personal testimony about how I see the role of government. It is obvious that there is a role for government in all this, but it is not the one which has been classified so crudely as either being a top-down or a bottom-up approach. I hope you will see a government which uses its authority to establish a framework but one which does encourage innovation on the ground. We are looking for institutional reform which directly benefits particular groups, but which is also part of a much wider transformation which represents social advance and social betterment.

To summarise briefly, I spoke about the rudimentary framework which we are establishing for welfare reform. It is clear that there are economic factors which account for the rise in welfare dependency here and elsewhere. There is also the interaction between how the welfare system now operates and its effect on behaviour, what I would call 'character'. Finally there is the cautionary side to the debate: that we are ceasing to live in a society where taxpayers let us put our hands in their pockets and take out more money.

The question is, given the size of the government budget, how do we use what we have much more effectively? Delivery of welfare will be determined by what we see as its nature and how we redefine that as we approach the millennium. It will also be determined by an approach which views welfare not as something neutral but as a means of social advance and social betterment. We have to decide what values welfare should teach and what values it should not.

Finally, I said there were strategies. To summarise, they are:

- the need to rebuild the coalition of support which used to exist for welfare – this will be determined in part by how successfully we answer the question about the nature of welfare
- the desire both to help people from dependency into opportunity, and to stop them reaching dependency in the first place

- the requirement of putting our initial ideas before the country for debate, in a manner reminiscent of Lloyd George, rather than finalising the ideas in private
- the requirement that our reforms be rooted firmly in society rather than imposed on it and that we appeal to those organisations, and collections of individuals, who, by furthering their own interests, can promote the common good as well.

Chapter 10:
Nicholas Timmins

We have been at welfare reform for centuries. Long before Beveridge we started with Elizabethan poor law, went through the Victorian version and on to Lloyd George. Throughout this time the central problems have remained the same: how to provide both adequate protection for all – particularly for the poor and less well-equipped – while preserving and ideally improving incentives both to work and to save. This is worth mentioning because the problems all societies are currently grappling with in terms of their welfare systems, including industrialising societies as well developed industrial ones, are long-standing and, in many ways, fairly intractable.

In the United Kingdom, up to the mid-1970s, efforts at welfare reform tended to involve spending more taxpayers' money in developing first and second pensions, attempts to reform both the tax and benefit system, and ways of creating more efficient labour markets. The introduction of earnings-related additions to unemployment benefits in the 1960s, for example – a move at that time supported by both Labour and the Conservatives – was an attempt to make the employment shake-out from declining or over-manned industries, the downsizing of the 1960s, more tolerable. People were encouraged to accept change in much the same way as in the 1980s and 1990s when pensions funds were used to encourage early retirement. So the problems or the dilemmas change very little, even if the policy prescriptions become very different over time.

The turning point in policy terms came in the mid-1970s, in the wake of the oil price rise, at the very time, so it turns out, that Britain's welfare state broadly stablised. Since that time combined spending on the major programmes – social security, health, education, housing, personal social services – has remained in the range of 20 to 23 per cent of GDP, a little above that figure in recessions, a little bit below during booms.

Until the mid-1970s, economic growth and faith in state-provided services allowed successive governments to increase public spending to itself, while at the same time leaving taxpayers with more discretionary spending of their own; a trend which continued well into the 1980s in continental Europe, where growth rates were higher. As the British economy began to stagnate, a greater reluctance to pay taxes set in.

At the same time, the broadly stable level of welfare spending has hidden significant changes in its distribution. These changes have been driven in part by rising numbers of the elderly, a smaller school age population – offset by rising numbers entering higher education – and marked shifts in the numbers of unemployed people and lone parents reliant on benefits. Direct spending on social housing has declined dramatically, offset by a sharp increase in spending on housing benefit. Health, as measured by NHS spending, has increased its share of GDP by about one-fifth, up from around 5 per cent of GDP in the mid-1970s to nearer 6 per cent now. Education spending, as a share of GDP, has remained remarkably constant, despite the number of people in higher education more than doubling.

The changing distribution of spending and the demographics of an ageing population have helped to create the growing impression of a public sector under strain, though those who think that this sense of crisis is unique might do well to read their history: the welfare state has always lived in a climate of unease about its future and, whatever happens from now on, I suspect it always will.

Moving from the wider welfare state to the issue of welfare itself there have broadly been three major reforms of social security since the mid-1970s. Incidentally, I do not think that the Americanisation of the language has helped the debate here, because it roughly categorises 'welfare' as bad and 'social security' as good, which has muddled rather than clarified some of the arguments in this country.

The first reform was the first Conservative government's decision to get rid of all the earnings-related additions and to break the link between pensions and earnings, raising the value of the basic state pension and unemployment benefit in line only with prices. That first large decision has cut current levels of spending on state pensions by between £7 and £8 billion a year – a major short-term saving, driven partly by public spending considerations, but also, in the case of the unemployment benefit, by worries about replacement ratios.

Next came Norman Fowler's review of social security in the mid-1980s, which took a hard look at most, but not all, of the benefit system. Critically he was prevented by the then Chancellor, Nigel Lawson, from looking in any meaningful way at the interaction of tax and benefits. This limitation lessened the impact of his reforms. He produced some important technical changes to benefits, which got rid of the worst of the poverty trap, but his most substantial change was the long-term one – halving the out-turn costs, and therefore the benefits to be paid out under SERPS, the State Earnings Related Pension Scheme. Fowler also introduced personal pensions, the first big privatisation of social security in Britain.

This was followed by Peter Lilley's five-year reign as Secretary of State for Social Security from 1992. Whatever his critics may say of him, Peter Lilley developed a clear strategy for tackling his £70 billion budget, as it was then, very early on. He worked through the social security budget sector by sector introducing a plethora of changes, the most dramatic of which was a further halving of the cost of SERPS plus a series of measures which tightened eligibility to a whole range of benefits from housing and disability benefits to those paid to the unemployed.

The impact on expenditure has been dramatic. In the long term, according to the government actuary, National Insurance contributions could actually fall in the next century and still pay for the existing pension system. In the short term, if the Department of Social Security's projections are to be believed, the social security budget is actually set to grow below the rate of the economy as a whole up to the year 2000.

The broad picture, therefore, on the United Kingdom's position internationally is not bad. We do face rising spending pressures from an ageing population; they are distinctly limited pressures between now and 2011, but will increase sharply from then until 2040 or so. But compared to the picture in many other countries – France, Germany and Japan, to name but three – the United Kingdom's position from the point of view of ageing is better than most. In considerable measure we have got some of the ageing in early. In addition, by the standards of many developed countries, our spending on both welfare and the welfare state remains low, as does our tax take, at 36 per cent of GDP.

The problem is that hardly anyone seems satisfied with this outcome. The total Social Security bill, including administration, will still top £100 billion next year. There are still large numbers of unemployed youngsters and long-term unemployed, plus 1 million lone parents on benefit. The very success of restraining both the short and long-term budgets has created renewed issues about adequacy, most notably over pensions, but also in other parts of the system. In addition to that, there is the cross-party agreement that, as the Prime Minister said recently, we have reached the limits of the public's willingness simply to fund an unreformed welfare system through ever higher taxes and benefits. Furthermore, reducing the social security budget could be the source of new money for education and health. So where do we go?

The answer has been that everybody is having to learn from everybody else's welfare programmes: Australia's GEP, California's GAIN, America's America Works.

With the Conservatives there was a string of initiatives from Work Start to Work Wise and most recently Project Work – the closest Britain has come to genuine Workfare. This is targeted at the very long-term unemployed, those out of work for two years or more, providing them with thirteen weeks assisted job search, followed by thirteen weeks compulsory work. The scheme, originally a pilot launched only last April with 8,000 places, has rapidly expanded, and was rapidly expanded by the Conservatives ahead of the general election to provide 100,000 places. This was not because it proved stunningly successful at getting people back to work but because large numbers, 30 per cent or more, left the Register when confronted with the time-consuming prospect of turning up for work. The assumption being they were claiming benefit but in fact working. At present, as far as we know this assumption that people were claiming while working remains an assumption. We do not know yet, though there is some research underway which is yet to report, what actually became of these people; whether they were in fact indulging in straight fraud, or whether they were transferring to other benefits, had moved away or found jobs.

Although much of the focus had been on employment benefits and jobs, one of the more intractable parts of the benefit system in recent years has been claims for sickness and disability – a section of the budget where claims continue to rise. I think the academic evidence on this is not good either way, but there must be at least a suspicion that there is a balloon effect here. As unemployment benefits become tougher to claim, more people are finding ways to qualify for disability benefits.

In terms of motivation, persuading someone who has been allocated sickness benefit back into work seems likely to be a tougher proposition than merely getting someone classified as unemployed back into the job market. Once labelled as 'unfit for work' the psychological barriers to returning to work must be greater.

In addition, in recent years we have seen the relative

success of Family Credit in helping lone mothers and some families back into work – some 700,000 claimants now – and the pilot scheme, known as 'Earnings Top Up', which will in effect pay family credit at a lower rate to those without children. This scheme is rightly being piloted because no one is sure what its labour market effects will be.

Finally, as a legacy from the Conservative government, there are proposals for Parent Plus, which allows the private sector to take on lone parents and help them find work, and the more radical idea involving the private sector to deliver contracts for work for the longer-term unemployed. Again, like Project Work, this is likely to be a compulsory scheme.

Into this comes the new government's plan for Welfare to Work, a vastly more ambitious programme directed along similar lines; one where the broad outline is clear, but where many details remain to be spelt out – not least whether the Conservative plans for Parent Plus and the contract for work will still go ahead within that new framework. With this, no doubt, will come a further assault on fraud.

The discovery of benefit fraud is one of the notable events of recent years. Everyone always knew it existed, but the work Peter Lilley commissioned while at the Department of Social Security, and the voracity with which Frank Field pursued the issue when Chair of the Commons Social Security Committee, showed there was a great deal more fraud than most people had imagined. Whether it remotely reaches some of the more exaggerated estimates – a housing beneficial loan, for example – remains to be seen. But tackling fraud is clearly important in order to build integrity into the social security system. While it will produce savings, however,I doubt if it will provide an absolute goldmine in terms of reducing the benefit bill.

A distinguishing feature of all the programmes – the Welfare to Work aspect, the contract work and all the others – is that they involve spending money up front in the hope of making savings later. Whether they will is an argument more for the economist than for me. But it is clear that in the short term, while the reforms may reduce the benefit bill they will not reduce public spending. This will only come if the schemes deliver lasting improvements in the job prospects for those failed by the education system or who have found themselves out of work for long periods of time: the latter, by definition, the hardest group to reconnect to work.

The one significant change in the new Labour government has been their determination to look at the problem in the round. The appointment of a minister actually charged with long-term thinking about the welfare state has to be an improvement. The announcement that Martin Taylor, Chief Executive of Barclays, is to head a task-force looking at reform of the tax and benefit system is as clear a signal as there could be that Labour is serious about what some see as the Holy Grail of benefit reform: a more integrated tax and benefit system. By no means the least important part of that announcement is that civil servants from the Inland Revenue, DSS, Treasury and the Department for Education and Employment will be seconded to a task-force.

It is worth remembering that the 1964 Labour government and the 1974 Conservative government both started out with similar brave ambitions. Both largely failed to deliver. One reason was simple interdepartmental rivalry – the Inland Revenue had no interest in the payment of benefits, only in tax collection. The other was that almost all, if not all, of the reforms proposed in the past in this area have proved expensive – either in revenue foregone, as the tax take at the lower end is reduced, or in high expenditure, as the tapers by which benefits are withdrawn as earnings rise are made more generous. It may well be that integrating tax and benefits will not be a route to saving money. Nonetheless, it has to be right to have another try. In doing so the Labour government is at least attempting what the last government, with all its proclaimed radicalism, never actually tried – looking at the system in the round.

If getting the unemployed back into work is important, at least as important in the long run is an attempt to undo or at least mitigate a system which encourages partners with low or part-time earnings to give up work when the main breadwinner loses their job, i.e. the perverse incentives which have helped reduce the widening divide between work-rich and work-poor households. All this could well produce a better and more economically productive benefit system. What I am not at all sure about is that it will produce a cheaper one, or at least a cheaper one in its overall effect on the government's finances.

This brings me to the other areas of welfare where I suspect the big political divide will lie – quite probably within Labour, as well as between the parties. One issue is whether the aim is really to cut the tax burden much further and genuinely get public spending down as a share of GDP, or whether it is to shift the boundaries of who pays what, in which way, and how far people should be compelled to make provision for themselves.

In pensions the big issue which sits alongside the public spending one is the issue of adequacy. Conservative performance may have cut the long-term bill, but large numbers of people are saving too little privately for their pension, given that the basic state pension on present policies is set to fall from its present 15 per cent of average earnings to 7 per cent or 8 per cent by 2040. Here Peter Lilley's dramatic plan to privatise the whole system for a new generation of workers does not, it seems to me, hold the answer. Radical undoubtedly, and technically brilliant, it seems to be absolutely the right answer to the wrong question. It produces dramatic savings in benefit expenditure but only after 2040, at the moment, when on present projections, the worse of the so-called demographic crisis begins to pass us by. On the way it involves extra expenditure in rebates, whose cost will rise inexorably to £7 billion a year over the very period when the public spending problems in health, education, social services and elsewhere in the welfare state will be at their most acute. It also, incidentally, requires an enormous statement of faith; that future chancellors, forty years down the road, will leave the pension pay-outs untaxed – a change Peter Lilley had to introduce to reduce the rebate bill from £15 million a year and make the scheme workable. For these reasons privatising the basic state pension in this way looks to be a step too far.

Further private provision of second-tier pensions, however, does make sense. But the main issue will be whether this can be achieved without greater compulsion – greater compulsion lower down the income scale than at present.

Frank Field's conclusion, in his final personal report as Chairman of the Commons Social Security Committee, was that this was indeed necessary. For it to work the taxpayer should contribute for those citizens genuinely unable to pay, for care of the long-term sick and the genuinely unemployed. It will be interesting, to put it mildly, to see how that argument plays out in government. This leaves the other big ticket items: health and education.

Education is everyone's priority. The schools are crying out for cash and universities are screaming for it. So Ron Dearing's review of higher education funding looks a racing certainty to recommend some form of loan system, probably secured in the private sector, to cover all student maintenance, possibly extending to tuition fees as well.

But there are many bidders for the cash. First, the universities themselves, whose funding problems will not be solved unless they get the money; second, pre-school and school education; third, there are plenty of other people who can think of ways to spend £1.2 billion if they can get their hands on it – Mr. Field recently suggested it should go to provide childcare to help parents back into work. What is certain is that loans covering maintenance will be the thick end of a larger wedge, which is likely to stretch first into higher education tuition and possibly later into post-sixteen and further education, perhaps underwritten by a voucher.

The remaining significant issue is health. This is most intractable for those seeking private sector solutions, both because the issue is genuinely difficult and because the NHS remains the most sacred of the British welfare state sacred cows. To maintain its position, more will progressively have to be spent on it. It is the area politicians of all parties are least willing to tackle. But it is also the one where private provision can come most easily by default.

To switch to private schooling involves individuals leaving the state sector entirely and paying fees out of post-tax income. In health, individuals can mix and match, using the private sector for one particular operation while still having access to the NHS when they need it for other things.

The introduction of new charges for the NHS − hospital stays or GP visits, for example − would be a major political step. Greater private provision by individuals, leading to the progressive development of a genuinely two-tier service, could well happen in stages if the complicated sums over government spending priorities do not yield up more money for the NHS in the coming years. It is particularly a short-term problem for the Health Service, given the wondrously tight spending plans to which the government is committed. But this is also a longer-term problem.

To sum up, on welfare reform in action we have reached the position where the issue is less one of absolute affordability or adequacy than of how to cope with genuine difficulties in unemployment, involving not just those out of work and registered as such but, as with many lone parents, people who are out of the labour market but would like to be in it.

There will be a distinct shift towards a safety net provision in social security, with help increasingly becoming conditional upon active job-searching – work of one sort or another – and a significant argument over compulsion in pensions.

I believe we are heading for a system in which public spending services are going to gradually narrow down onto the core of the welfare state: health, schooling and the safety net, with graduates increasingly required to repay their educational costs over their lifetime. How far this will hold will depend, at least in the short term, on whether the government convinces the electorate that it is making the system work better, and that spending money on Welfare to Work is actually achieving something of benefit both to the individuals concerned and to the broader society. If it can do that, it can then go on to make the case for higher government spending on health, education and keeping people linked to the labour market.

Chapter 11:
Evan Davis

David Willetts once likened the social security system to car insurance and asked what would happen if, instead of having compulsory car insurance, we prohibited car insurance? He observed that we would probably have safer driving, but on the unfortunate occasions when accidents did occur – and there would be considerably fewer accidents – it would be a terrible catastrophe for those involved.

One might be forgiven for thinking that this is the alternative to the current social security system which we are being offered. We can clearly reduce the number of single parents or unemployed people by reducing the protection we offer them but only at the expense of increasing the penalty for those who unwittingly fall into single parenthood or into unemployment.

Rather than confining ourselves to this stark choice I would like to address an issue that lies behind much of the current debate about welfare reform; an issue on which there has been almost no explicit discussion in this country and that to some extent allows you to find a third way between leaving the unlucky uninsured and the wilful over-insured. The issue is eligibility and the conditions we attach to the receipt of social security benefits.

To Peter Lilley's credit, virtually every reform he presented to the last parliament involved the question of eligibility and the introduction of a greater discrimination within the system between categories of recipient. Housing Benefit reforms were designed to ensure that money did not go to people who were living in places which were larger than their needs. Incapacity Benefit reforms improved the test which determined people's ability to work. The introduction of Job Seekers' Allowances placed the onus very clearly on people who are claiming benefits genuinely to seek work. Despite these measures, eligibility remains a much under-discussed issue which cuts to the heart of the way we administer our benefit system.

For one thing it solves the car insurance problem I mentioned earlier. It is clear that no one wants all dangerous drivers thinking, 'I can do what I want because I'm insured'. We do not want uninsured drivers who, although very careful, end up suffering personal catastrophe because they are unlucky. What is needed is an insurance system which in effect says that if you were driving dangerously you do not get your insurance pay-out, but if you were driving perfectly safely then you do.

The right eligibility criteria improve the system in a number of ways. They deliver a clear financial benefit by reducing the number of people receiving a pay-out who do not need assistance – this should be a priority whether the social security system is in crisis or not. They also solve a lot of so-called 'moral hazard' problems by removing incentives to misbehave. Furthermore, they help politically by addressing the lack of legitimacy which arises when the general public believes money is being paid out to people who are not in genuine need.

Finally, refining eligibility criteria helps address a fundamental problem in social security design; how to get rid of the poverty trap. I have spent many years of my life at the Institute for Fiscal Studies looking at ways of diminishing or removing the poverty trap. The IFS were blunt about the prospects for success. In a book it published about ten years ago called *The Reform of Social Security* it asked:

> Do we need to institutionalise the poverty trap, as we
> expect our critics will observe? Can high marginal tax
> rates on the poor be avoided? We are forced reluctantly
> to conclude that they cannot. We have seen no practical
> scheme which avoids this difficulty, except by accepting
> a worse evil; substantial reductions in the level of support
> for the poor, or very high marginal tax rates on a much
> higher proportion of the population.

For those who have ever spent any time working on social
security, this is what you find when you attempt to reform it.
You say, 'Isn't it terrible? All these poor people at the bottom
with very high marginal rates. Let's tinker with this. Let's
tinker with that.' It is like squeezing a balloon. You either
find yourself squeezing the high marginal rates further up
the income distribution, or cutting benefit levels and
penalising people in order to clear them from high marginal
rates, undermining the whole purpose for which the system
was established in the first place.

Of course, this impossibility theorem of social security
reform only holds true if eligibility is uniform and based
solely on people's means. If you say to people, 'You could do
better for yourself than you currently are, and thus we are
not going to award you benefits on your actual income.
Instead, we are going to award them to you on the basis of
what we think your income should be, or what your income
could be if you were trying hard enough', then the whole
problem disappears. In principle, then, eligibility is a tool

with considerable moral, financial and technical advantages. Unfortunately, it is also a very difficult thing to change and a very difficult thing to talk about.

Traditionally, the Right has not been especially interested in eligibility, focusing more on privatising welfare provision rather than reforming it, even though privatisation *per se* does nothing to solve the moral hazard problems. The Left has fought shy of eligibility because it involves making a distinction between what one might call the 'deserving' and the 'undeserving' poor. They have construed any attack on fraudulent or unhelpful payments, and on payments to people who were complicit in their own downfall, as an attack on the whole basis of welfare. Somewhere in the middle are the technocrats like the IFS, who have never had any interest in this area because the judgements about deserving versus undeserving, or wilful versus unwilful, do not fit neatly into their models.

Yet in addressing the issue of eligibility, we must start to ask new questions about the future shape of our social security system. Let me briefly look at some of them.

Should benefit officers tend to follow rules, or should they be given more discretion? One of the advantages of discretionary systems is that benefit officers know more about the people they are dealing with than the state and thus eligibility is easier to assess. But, as a nation, we have tended to avoid using this knowledge. Instead we have a complex set of universal rules. That is why, to claim Incapacity Benefit you have to pass a labourious test which includes pointless questions about whether you can pick up a pen and drop it from a height of a foot, rather than having an interview with a benefit officer who can clearly say, 'Look, I know you cannot be a miner, but you could be a filing clerk and I know various jobs that are available.'

What is clear is that informal systems of administering welfare work better than those bound by rules. Let us look at the extended family as an example. Within its confines everyone is personally accountable for their behaviour and everyone knows who has been shirking and who is simply down on their luck. Because of the discipline implied by monitoring which goes within this informal social network, there is very little in the way of bad behaviour or moral hazard relative to our social security system. Small social security systems, systems that operate across groups of fifty people – people who are essentially on first name terms – probably work better than systems that work across units the size of Brent. The Kibbutz, for instance, probably works better than the DSS as a system of informal monitoring.

Are there other ways? There could, for example, be cover provided to groups of individuals and each group could be allowed to allocate their benefit receipts themselves on the basis of their own informal monitoring of who deserves and who does not deserve to receive benefit. If there are going to be much tougher eligibility requirements, and people are going to be told, 'I am sorry, you have got yourself into this. We do not pay out for people who get into this', what back-up system is there? You clearly cannot literally throw the single mother with her child onto the streets and say, 'Beg for your existence'. You clearly have to have some other secondary safety net for those who miss the original. What kind of system does that need to be? Are we talking about homeless shelters and soup kitchens? Or, are we saying that actually we are not willing to countenance any of those, so there is no point in being tough in eligibility requirements? Obviously, if there is no question of taking benefits away from people, there is little point in discussing this further.

These are just two interesting questions. I do not believe that the debate about reforming social security in this country has gone nearly as far as it could. I believe there are probably far more able-bodied people of working age drawing benefits than there needs to be. I also believe that it is mistaken to think that 20 per cent or 30 per cent of the population needs to live in housing designated for low income groups.

There is a project out there if anyone has the courage to grasp it. It is not about privatising the welfare state – though it may involve an element of privatisation – it is about moving on from the defensive, and frankly, rather naive beliefs which have typified the Left's traditional approach to the social security system and examining some of the issues I have presented here.

I hope that when Frank Field and his colleagues look at the files in the DSS they see that there is much which can and should be done. Most of all I hope that the debate over the next few years, conducted in a spirit of compassion and toughness, provides very practical ideas about how to distinguish between those categories of people who should not be supported by the taxpayer and those who should.

Chapter 12:
Tim Hames

Much has been made of the essentially similar problems which the welfare systems of the United Kingdom and United States face, but similar problems do not necessarily mean similar causes or similar solutions. In fact, I would argue that the scope for transferring welfare models between America and Britain is relatively modest.

For all of the similarities between the two countries, for instance the character of the business cycle and labour market flexibility, a very large degree of caution needs to be exercised when attempting to transplant policy ideas from the United States into a British context. There are three main reasons for this.

The first is that in contrast to the field of economics, the structure, culture and historical evolution of our two welfare states are highly distinctive. These distinctions show themselves in a variety of ways.

As Robert Skidelsky has reminded us, a socialist and redistributive ethos runs through the British welfare state in a way it does not in America. So in Britain, universal entitlements sit alongside means-tested benefits, whereas in the United States the welfare system tends to target worthy groups such as veterans, the elderly, the disabled and children almost regardless of whether or not they are actually poor. This leads to the rather perverse consequence that over half of all American transfer payments go to people of average incomes or above; primarily the consequence of Medicare. Yet outside of social security and Medicare, the middle-class are largely out of the American welfare and benefit system. This means that public opinion is much more instinctively hostile to the very term 'welfare' in America than in Britain.

It makes good politics to be an anti-welfare politician in America – despite a twenty point lead in the polls in September 1996 Bill Clinton was persuaded to sign a Welfare Reform Bill he did not like because of the political consequences if he did not. Compare this to the sorry story of the Back to Basics enterprise in Britain.

Underlying these differences is, I think, the most important one. In the United States the role of religion – especially the Protestant religion and the Protestant work ethic – is considerably stronger than in any European country and probably any other major nation state in the world. The ingrained belief in meritocracy, the belief that if only you give yourself the opportunity you can achieve, is so much higher than is sadly still the case in Britain.

If the cultural and historical evolution of the two welfare systems gives pause for thought, so should the differences in their delivery and administration. There remains a much larger element of non-governmental provision in the United States than in Britain and what counts as governmental is divided between the federal state and local levels in a way that does not have a direct parallel in Britain. There is also the question of what these agencies deliver: in America benefits are more frequently paid in kind – for instance through food stamps – than offered as straight cash assistance. Enormous caution is required in comparing the two systems not least because of the size of administrative unit involved. Policy at the American national level is simply too large to be thought of sensibly as a model for Britain. Even after the Americans have begun moving towards a more decentralised system following the Welfare Reform

Act of 1996, considerable care is required in selecting one's state of choice.

You need to start with states which are a reasonable size and which have comparable urban populations. You also need to recognise that in America there is an extremely powerful and distinctive connection between race and the urban underclass which simply does not have a parallel in Britain. This means excluding states where race is an overbearing factor because, by American standards, they have a disproportionately large number of non-white residents. Crucially, of course, states also need to be doing something interesting and radical in welfare reform.

There are probably twenty American states large enough by population to suit our needs. Of these, fourteen have a black and Hispanic population which is 50 per cent higher than the American national average, and a further three, Massachusetts, Michigan and New Jersey, have large cities whose conditions are not really applicable in Britain. Two more, Indiana and Minnesota, have done little that is interesting by American standards in terms of welfare reform. This leaves you with one state, Wisconsin. It is the right sort of size, it is not overly biased by race and it is actually engaged in reform worth looking at as James Miller has already made clear.

Of course, Wisconsin does not have a monopoly on welfare reform wisdom. There are models in Australia, Canada and New Zealand which are all worthy of study. However, the best place to look for hints about how to proceed in reforming our welfare state is at ourselves.

Papers in Print

SMF Papers

1. The Social Market Economy
    Robert Skidelsky
    £3.50

2. Responses to Robert Skidelsky on the Social Market Economy
    Sarah Benton, Kurt Biedenkopf, Frank Field, Danny Finkelstein, Francis Hawkings,
    Graham Mather
    £3.50

3. Europe Without Currency Barriers
    Samuel Brittan, Michael Artis
    £5.00

4. Greening the White Paper: A Strategy for NHS Reform
    Gwyn Bevan, Marshall Marinker
    £5.00

5. Education and the Labour Market: An English Disaster
    Adrian Wooldridge
    £5.00

6. Crisis in Eastern Europe: Roots and Prospects
    Robin Okey
    £4.00

7. Fighting Fiscal Privilege: Towards a Fiscal Constitution
    Deepak Lal
    £4.00

8. Eastern Europe in Transition
    Clive Crook, Daniel Franklin
    £5.00

9. The Open Network and its Enemies:
    Towards a Contestable Telecommunications Market
    Danny Finkelstein, Craig Arnall
    £5.00

10. A Restatement of Economic Liberalism
Samuel Brittan
£5.00

11. Standards in Schools: Assessment, Accountability and the Purposes of Education
John Marks
£6.00

12. Deeper Share Ownership
Matthew Gaved, Anthony Goodman
£6.00

13. Fighting Leviathan: Building Social Markets that Work
Howard Davies
£6.00

14. The Age of Entitlement
David Willetts
£6.00

15. Schools and the State
Evan Davis
£6.00

16. Public Sector Pay: In Search of Sanity
Ron Beadle
£8.00

17. Beyond Next Steps: a Civil Service for the 1990s
Sir Peter Kemp
£8.00

18. Post-Communist Societies in Transition: A Social Market Perspective
John Gray
£8.00

19. Two Cheers for the Institutions
Stanley Wright
£10.00

20. Civic Conservatism
David Willetts
£10.00

21. The Undoing of Conservatism
John Gray
£10.00

34. Ready for Treatment
Nick Bosanquet and Stephen Pollard
£10.00

35. The Future of Welfare
ed. Roderick Nye
£10.00

Reports

1. Environment, Economics and Development after the 'Earth Summit'
Andrew Cooper
£3.00

2. Another Great Depression? Historical Lessons for the 1990s
Robert Skidelsky, Liam Halligan
£5.00

3. Exiting the Underclass: Policy towards America's Urban Poor
Andrew Cooper, Catherine Moylan
£5.00

4. Britain's Borrowing Problem
Bill Robinson
£5.00

Occasional Papers

1. Deregulation
David Willetts
£3.00

2. 'There is No Such Thing as Society'
Samuel Brittan
£3.00

3. The Opportunities for Private Funding in the NHS
David Willetts
£3.00

4. A Social Market for Training
Howard Davies
£3.00

5. Beyond Unemployment
Robert Skidelsky, Liam Halligan
£6.00

6. Brighter Schools
    Michael Fallon
    £6.00

7. Understanding 'Shock Therapy'
    Jeffrey Sachs
    £8.00

8. Recruiting to the Little Platoons
    William Waldegrave
    £6.00

9. The Culture of Anxiety: The Middle Class in Crisis
    Matthew Symonds
    £8.00

10. What is left of Keynes?
    Samuel Brittan, Meghnad Desai, Deepak Lal, Robert Skidelsky, Tom Wilson
    £8.00

11. Winning the Welfare Debate
    Peter Lilley (Introduction by Frank Field)
    £10.00

12. Financing the Future of the Welfare State
    Robert Skidelsky, Will Hutton
    £8.00

13. Picking Winners: The East Asian Experience
    Ian Little
    £8.00

14. Over-the-Counter Medicines
    Alan Maynard, Gerald Richardson
    £10.00

15. Pressure Group Politics in Modern Britain
    Riddell, Waldegrave, Secrett, Bazalgette, Gaines, Parminter
    £10.00

16. Design Decisions: Improving the Public Effectiveness of Public Purchasing
    Taylor, Fisher, Sorrell, Stephenson, Rawsthorn, Davis, Jenkins, Turner, Taylor
    £10.00

17. Stakeholder Society vs Enterprise Centre of Europe
    Robert Skidelsky, Will Hutton
    £10.00

18. Setting Enterprise Free
    Ian Lang
    £10.00

19. Community Values and the Market Economy
    John Kay
    £10.00

Other Papers

Local Government and the Social Market
George Jones
£3.00

Full Employment without Inflation
James Meade
£6.00

Memoranda

1. Provider Choice: 'Opting In' through the Private Finance Initiative
   Michael Fallon
   £5.00

2. The Importance of Resource Accounting
   Evan Davis
   £3.50

3. Why There is No Time to Teach:
   What is wrong with the National Curriculum 10 Level Scale
   John Marks
   £5.00

4. All Free Health Care Must be Effective
   Brendan Devlin, Gwyn Bevan
   £5.00

5. Recruiting to the Little Platoons
   William Waldegrave
   £5.00

6. Labour and the Public Services
   John Willman
   £8.00

7. Organising Cost Effective Access to Justice
Gwyn Bevan, Tony Holland and Michael Partington
£5.00

8. A Memo to Modernisers
Ron Beadle, Andrew Cooper, Evan Davis, Alex de Mont,
Stephen Pollard, David Sainsbury, John Willman
£8.00

9. Conservatives in Opposition: Republicans in the US
Daniel Finkelstein
£5.00

10. Housing Benefit: Incentives for Reform
Greg Clark
£8.00

11. The Market and Clause IV
Stephen Pollard
£5.00

12. Yeltsin's Choice: Background to the Chechnya Crisis
Vladimir Mau
£8.00

13. Teachers' Practices: A New Model for State Schools
Tony Meredith
£8.00

14. The Right to Earn: Learning to Live with Top People's Pay
Ron Beadle
£8.00

15. A Memo to Modernisers II
John Abbott, Peter Boone, Tom Chandos, Evan Davis, Alex de Mont, Ian Pearson MP,
Stephen Pollard, Katharine Raymond, John Spiers
£8.00

16. Schools, Selection and the Left
Stephen Pollard
£8.00

17. The Future of Long-Term Care
Andrew Cooper, Roderick Nye
£8.00

18. Better Job Options for Disabled People: Re-employ and Beyond
Peter Thurnham
£8.00

19. Negative Equity and the Housing Market
Andrew Cooper, Roderick Nye
£6.00

20. Industrial Injuries Compensation: Incentives to Change
Dr Greg Clark, Iain Smedley
£8.00

21. Better Government by Design: Improving the Effectiveness of Public Purchasing
Katharine Raymond, Marc Shaw
£8.00

22. A Memo to Modernisers III
Evan Davis, John Kay, Alex de Mont, Stephen Pollard, Brian Pomeroy,
Katharine Raymond
£8.00

23. The Citizen's Charter Five Years On
Roderick Nye
£8.00

24. Standards of English and Maths in Primary Schools for 1995
John Marks
£10.00

25. Standards of Reading, Spelling and Maths for 7-year-olds in Primary Schools for 1995
John Marks
£10.00

26. An Expensive Lunch: The Political Economy of Britain's New Monetary Framework
Robert Chote
£10.00

27. A Memo to Martin Taylor
David Willetts
£10.00

28. Why Fundholding Should Stay
David Colin-Thomé
£10.00

Trident Trust/ SMF Contributions to Policy

Hard Data

Centre for
Post-Collectivist Studies

1. Russia's Stormy Path to Reform
    Robert Skidelsky (ed.)
    £20.00

2. Macroeconomic Stabilisation in Russia: Lessons of Reforms, 1992–1995
    Robert Skidelsky, Liam Halligan
    £10.00

3. The End of Order
    Francis Fukuyama
    £9.50

Briefings

1. A Guide to Russia's Parliamentary Elections
    Liam Halligan, Boris Mozdoukhov
    £10.00